Chambal

revisited

Author and journalist Suvendu Debnath

Chambal
revisited

English rendering of
Suvendu Debnath's *Abar Chambal* by
NABANITA SENGUPTA

Hawakal
PUBLISHERS
New Delhi | Calcutta

HAWAKAL
New Delhi | Calcutta

HAWAKAL PUBLISHERS
70 B/9 Amritpuri, East of Kailash, New Delhi 65
33/1/2 K B Sarani, Mall Road, Calcutta 80

Email info@hawakal.com
Website www.hawakal.com

Cover designed by Bitan Chakraborty

First edition (paperback) February 2022

ISBN: 978-93-91431-03-7 (paperback)

Price: INR 450 | USD 19.99

for
ma'am
(Prof. Jharna Sanyal)

Translator's Note

Translation for me is an act of love. It is an act that makes a work transcend its linguistic borders to reach a wider audience. Reading Suvendu Debnath's *Abar Chambal* persuaded me to believe that this book needed to reach a larger community of readers. Hence the need to translate. The author has portrayed Chambal through myriad lenses—looking at it through economic, geographical, social, communal, and gender perspectives. His gaze is that of a seeker, a person who tries to understand a place by interacting with its inhabitants.

Chambal has remained an exotic name in our mindscape—with colourful images of dacoits on horses, violence and terror, and a mix of a Robinhoodian charm. This book engages with the real Chambal, a place consisting of actual human beings, and makes us realise that the problems, irrespective of their locations, largely remain the same in every society—greed for power and wealth, oppression of women, caste oppressions and so on. This book also makes us aware of the eternal struggle for existence, as we see the baghis finding ways to survive in spite of the police bullets and the harsh terrain. Even in this digital age, where technology dominates our lives and the world is changing faster than ever before,

Chambal with its caste politics, revenge killings and in-fighting, is in many ways stuck in an older world. As we proceed through the pages of this book, we come across a society which, growing up in close proximity of the ravines, seems to have imbibed its hostility and bleakness. But that's not all. If there is hostility, an urgency for revenge, there is also love and fellow feeling. The *baghis*, mostly born out of a sense of outrage at the injustices of the society, are not just dacoits. As Suvendu's interactions with them prove, they are also often the saviours for poor villagers so much so that *baghi* Mansingh is still revered in Chambal and also has a temple dedicated to him.

One important aspect of this book is the section on women baghis. Though the section occupies a smaller part of the book, it is extremely significant. An article, born out of Suvendu's stories on women baghis is now a part of an anthology of critical essays on women's displacement—*Understanding Women's Experiences of Displacement:Literature, Culture and Society in South Asia,* that I had co-edited and has been published by Routledge. This highlights the importance that this section has, and its importance in understanding women's experiences in the *beeheds.* Here we meet a bunch of women, forced by their fate, fearless and ferocious, eking out a life in the *beeheds* of Chambal. The portrayal of these women opens up a new discourse of gender studies and women's displacement. Most of these women, generally victims of rape and other abuses, are banished from their societies for no fault of theirs. Often, they are just pawns in the larger games of family feuds and revenges, as easy targets for family dishonour. They jump into the *beehed* to escape from the ruthlessness of their own societies, but even there, they become victims of gender abuses and marginalization. The extent of marginalization is so much that some baghis like Mohar Singh even refuse to acknowledge these women as baghis. Yet, there are others who not only accept them but also train them to lead this life in the *beeheds*. Putli Bai and Sultana's story is one of the biggest examples of this. "Feminism for me, has never been anti-men, it is anti-patriarchy"—these words of Kamla Bhasin assume greater significance in the lives of women baghis as we look at the dynamics of relationship between the male and female baghis of Chambal. I am sure this book will open up newer discourses on the empirical, socio-cultural, and gender issues prevalent in Chambal, as the book analyses these factors and their role in creating *baghis* out of peaceful, law-abiding inhabitants. I also believe that this book will be an important addition to the primary resources on Chambal, and will help readers achieve an engaged understanding of the region.

Nabanita Sengupta
6 February 2022
Calcutta

Acknowledgements

I express my gratitude to Suvendu Debnath for giving me this opportunity to translate his work, and for patiently awaiting its completion. A few more people who became my go-to persons and helped me in various ways are Subhajit Sengupta, Dr. Sudeshna Chakravorty, Aditi Banerjee, Dr. Tanmay Bir, and Dr. Sarbani Bhattacharya. Arpan Dasgupta had been a big help in correcting all the unintended typos. Sohini Chakrabarty kindly read through the entire manuscript. Gratitude is due, to the Hawakal Publishers, particularly Dr. Kiriti Sengupta and Bitan Chakraborty, for bringing out the fascinating book on Chambal in Bengali first and then being willing to publish its English translation. I am also grateful to Shamayita Sen for being such an insightful editor.

Our Book

A book is not the work of an author alone. Particularly a book of this kind is not a product of just the author's efforts. It carries blessings of its well-wishers, their encouragement, and reminders at every moment taking the work towards completion. Therefore, this book is not my book alone. If the editor of *Bhinnacharcha,* Ekram Ali, did not keep his faith in me, I could never have visited Chambal. Poet Ranjan Bandyopadhyay has instilled in me the knack for critical observation. The chief editor of *Bhinnocharcha* had sent me to Chambal and that has made writing about Chambal possible. Other colleagues such as Sudipto De and Santu Das have supported me at every step. The veteran journalist, Anurup Bhowmick, has given me perspectives and taught me the art of digging out information from people. And above all, there has been the author, Anil Ghosh, without whose encouragement I would never have joined journalism. He has scolded me for procrastinating and has chased me at every moment for the manuscript. I must specially mention poets, Atri Bhattacharya, and Abhishek Chakraborty. Both kept pressing me to complete the book, *Aabar Chambal.* Abhishek emphasised on the need to write a book such as this. I shared my work with Atri, who would often advise me regarding writing styles. Two more people whom I cannot fail to mention are Kiriti Sengupta and Bitan Chakraborty. For 15 days at a stretch, Kiriti *da* had put in his untiring efforts to publish this book. He has not only edited the book but also taught me a lot in the process. Bitan was there with words of encouragement—'Suvendu, keep on writing, I am sure you can do it.' I do not know how much readers will gain from this book, but authoring this has been an immense learning experience for me. This is not just my book, it belongs to all of them.

Suvendu Debnath
17 December, 2018
Calcutta

CURSED CHAMBAL

The name *beher*, or as the local Bundelkhand dialect goes, *beehed*, can make even the bravest of people quake with fear. The cursed river which has led to the creation of this *beehed* is called Chambal. Every bend of the river carries tales of injustice, torture, and exploitation. Its very origin seems to be in violence. It is not surprising that a river that has been cursed since its birth would carry deep marks of blood along its vast expanse. Right from the beginning, River Chambal has been bearing enmity, and that alone has given birth to its infamous law—an eye for an eye. The Chambal basin is heavy with various tales of exploitation of the poor by the rich, domination of the weak by the powerful, and revolts against the said injustices.

The creation of Chambal valley has an interesting tale too. The word Chambal is of Dravidian origin and it means fish. Flowing through the middle of *beehed*, covering approximately 900 kilometres, the beautiful and cleanest river of India, Chambal, crosses Mou, Gwalior, Bhind, Murena, Jalaon, Kanpur, and Kota on its way. This is the only river in India which is pollution-free. But neither human beings nor creatures drink its water because this river carries a curse since its birth. This river has been mentioned both in the Puranas and the Mahabharata. According to popular belief, Kauravas after defeating Pandavas in the game of dice had attempted to strip Draupadi on the bank of this river near Murana. Outraged, Draupadi had then cursed the river to bring woe to anyone drinking or using its water. Thus, there were very few settlements along the bank of this river. That is the reason for the river being sparkling clean even in the 21st century. According to experts, River Chambal is also the cause of death for many dacoits. Since it is the only source of drinking water, it makes dacoits susceptible to the police. After the Behmai incident, Phoolan Devi too had to spend a few days in the *beehed* without any water. It was out of extreme thirst that she thought of surrendering.

In India, all rivers originate in the north and flow down to the south but Chambal flows in the opposite direction. It flows from south to north. The origin of Chambal is in the Janapau hills, 616 metres above sea level, near the district of Mou in Madhya Pradesh. It flows in the north-east direction, crossing Dhar, Ujjaini, Ratlam, and Mandsaur districts before entering Rajasthan near Churasigarh. In Rajasthan, this river flows approximately 210 kilometres along Kota, Sawai Madhopur, and Dhaulpur districts. The length of the entire river is 966 kilometres. In its last leg, it flows through Itawa, Jalaon, and the rural areas of Kanpur before merging with the Yamuna. The tributaries of Chambal are Shipra, Sindh, Kalisindh, and Kunno or Kumari river. All these rivers flow in the northern or north-central part of India, crossing various districts of Madhya Pradesh and Rajasthan. Before turning south to meet the Yamuna in Uttar Pradesh, Chambal demarcates the boundary between Madhya Pradesh and Rajasthan. In these three states of India, Chambal is of immense importance. At present, there are four hydroelectric power stations upon this river—Gandhi Sagar, Rana Pratap Sagar, Jahar Sagar, and Kota Barrage.

Chambal's references in the times of the Purana and the Mahabharata are quite intriguing. The ancient name of this cursed river is 'Chamaravati' or 'Charmanvati.' The Aryans have always looked down upon this river because of the story of its origin. The story is both interesting as well as controversial. Narrating such a story in present times might make one a victim of political violence but how can one ignore one's past! At a short distance from Chambal was the town of Daspur. It was ruled by the great king Rantidev belonging to Raghuvansa. According to the story in Mahabharata, he performed the *Goyalambh* or *Gomedh yajna*. In this huge *yajna*, thousands of cows were sacrificed. It is said that when the hides of those cows were hung to dry, water dripped from those hides and formed the river Chambal; hence the name Charmanvati. It is said in the Chambal valley that this river is considered impious because of its origin from the hides of cows.

mahānadī carmarāśerutkaledāt sasṛje yataḥ
tataścarma ṇvatītvevaṁ vikhyātā sā mahānadī II
(santi parva 29/23)

(According to this *shloka*, the drippings from the hides had led to the creation of a huge river which came to be known as Charmanvati or Chambal).

In the Mahabharata, King Rantidev has been referred to as the king who had killed the cows.

rajño mahānase pūrve rantidevasya vai dvija
ahanyahani vadhyete dve sahasre gavāṁ tathā II
(vana parva 208/4) II

This event also finds mention in Rahul Sanskritayan's book, *From Volga to Ganga*. In another edition of the Mahabharata, blood that flowed due to sacrificing cows led to the formation of the river. This is not the end, there are more references to Chambal in Mahabharata.

tatas'carmaṇvavatī kule jambhakasyātmajam'
nṛpam' dadars'a vāsudevena s'eṣitam' pūrvavairiṇa II
(sabha parva, 31st adhyaya)

The *shloka* above means, after this (in the context of Sahadev's winning procession towards South), Sahadev finds Jambhak's son on the banks of Charmanvati, as he had been left alive by his earlier foe, Basudev. Sahadev defeats him in the battle and proceeds southwards.

Apart from this, in the pilgrimage episode in the *Vana Parva,* Charmanvati has been mentioned as a sacred river as it says:

carmaṇvati samāsādaya niyato niyatāsana
rantidevābhyayanu jñātamagniṣtomaphalaḥ labhet

In Mahabharata, in Ashwanadi's Charmanvati river, there is a mention of Charmanvati meeting Yamuna, and Yamuna finally meeting Ganga.

mañjuṣātvas'vanadayaḥ sā yayo carmāṇvatī nadīm'
carmāṇvatyāsva yamuna tato gaṇgā jagāmaha I
gaṅgāyāḥ sutaviṣaye campāmanuyayopurīm' I

On the other hand, even in the Srimadbhagawat Gita, Chambal or Charmanvati has been mentioned along with river Narmada—

surasanarmadā carmaṇvatī sindhurandha I

This was the story from Mahabharata. Chambal has made a place for itself in ancient literature as well. Even the great poet Kalidas could not resist describing the beauty of the river Chambal. I am quoting a few lines of the great poet here, along with an explanation of those lines—

Meghdut—Purva megha 48
ārādhyainam' s'aravaṇabhavam' devamullaṅghitādhvā
siddhadvandvairjalakaṇabhayadvīṇibhirmuktamārgaḥ I

valyamvethaḥ surabhitanayālaṃbhajām̐ mānayiṣyan
srotomūrttya bhuvi pariṇatam̐ rantidevasya kīrtim̐ II

(After worshipping Kartikeya, you will proceed towards the earth. The wise men with their wives, *veena* in hand, will stand aside to give you the way. You will come down to the earth to pay your respect to Carmavati river which has originated due to the *gomedh yajna* by the great king Rantidev.)

Purva megha 49
tvayyādātum̐ jalamavanate śārṅgiṇo varṇacaure
tasyāḥ sindhoḥ prithumapi tanum̐ dūrabhāvāt pravāham̐ I
prekṣiṣyante gaganatayo nūnamāvarjya driṣṭī
rekam̐ muktāguṇamiva bhuvaḥ sthūlamadhyendranīlam̐ II

(You too are dark-skinned like Krishna. When you will bow down to gather water from the river, the Wise Ones from above will see a blue gem in the middle of a string of white pearls. Though the river is voluminous, the distance from which they see it reduces it in size.)

Purva megha 50
tāmuttīrya braja paricitabhrūlatāvibhramāṇām̐
pakṣotkṣepāduparivilasatkṛṣṇaśāraprabhāṇām̐ I
Kundakṣepānugamadhukaraśrimuṣāmātmavimbam̐
pātrīkurvan daśāpurabadhūnetrakautūhalanām̐ II

(You shall reach Daspur on crossing Carmavati where the women are known for their art of dalliance using skills of arched eyebrows. Their eyes are as beautiful as the blackbuck. And when they raise their beautiful eyes, it seems as if a string of bumblebees are fluttering over star jasmines.)

So, there are plenty of evidences to prove that Chambal is an ancient river. But what is a *beehed*? In a layman's language, *beehed* would mean uneven land formed due to the river basin. These *beeheds* occupy most of the river basin of Chambal.

Along the path of River Chambal, there are either huge holes or uneven mounds. Some of them are as high as a double storey building, some just as tall as a human being; some contain natural tunnels, while at other places, the walking space between the mounds is extremely narrow. Except for a few thorny plants or those that grow on saline soil, no other vegetation is visible here. This area is quite similar to the Grand Canyon of United States of America, or the Gunguni region in our very own Garbeta, but the *beehed* is more extensive.

Beehed is responsible for the poverty and poor economic condition of this region. Chambal is not just famous for the river. From 1950s to 2015, Chambal has been famous for its *baghis* or dacoits. Right from the beginning, the basin has been under the clutches of dacoits or *baghis*. In common parlance, *baghi* means one who protests. They are the ones who were forced to pick up weapons to protest the wrongdoings and injustice, and take shelter in the thorny bush infested uneven valleys of Chambal.

Historically, the first recorded *baghi* of the *beehed* of Chambal was Samant Mahasen of the Batsya family in Rajasthan. He became a *baghi* due to his revolt against King Bhoj who had unfairly taken his rights away. So Mahasen started attacking Bhoj merchants when they returned from Gujarat, robbing them of their wealth. He built small fortresses along the *beehed* where he stationed his soldiers. The obsession to get back his rights had turned Mahasen into a cruel murderer. He became so cruel that people started using *Chand* as a prefix to his name. Though King Bhoj had sent soldiers to capture Mahasen multiple times, but due to the peculiar topography of *beehed*, the king never succeeded. Finally, Raja Bhoj sought help from Tomar clan, which had come from Delhi and settled near Chambal, to free them from the atrocities of Chand Mahasen. In return, Raja Bhoj promised the Tomar ruler, Bajrat Tomar, right to collect taxes. Tomar soldiers, used to the terrain of *beehad*, surrounded Chand from all sides and stayed put for fifteen days. Scarcity of water pushed almost all of Chand's companions to death, and Chand was killed by the Tomar soldiers. Tomars were rulers of Delhi before it was ruled by the Chauhan dynasty.

In Chambal, the period of modern dacoits, the *baghis*, begins from the 12th century. In those days, the Rajput king, Prithviraj Chauhan, was the ruler of Delhi. But then began the internal feuds among the Rajputs and Prithviraj exiled the Tomars from Delhi. The Tomars then took shelter in the *beehed* region of Chambal. They established their settlements in Bhind, Morena, and Datiya regions. But the Tomar Rajputs could not accept this insult. Prithviraj was a Rajput too. Tomars kept attacking Delhi repeatedly but failed each time. Each time they attacked Prithviraj's army, Chambal water turned incarnadine. Such bloodshed continued through Prithviraj's lifetime. Prithviraj died and Tomars also lost their power. Though head of both sides died, the enmity continued through successive generations. Short skirmishes continued. That was the beginning of Chambal's law—blood for blood. Thereafter, rulers in Delhi changed but, Tomars continued their attacks. Towards the end, this desire to win Delhi somehow turned into banditry. To survive in the *beehed* region one needed money and the easiest source of earning was robbery. Thus began the fights between smaller clans—Rajputs against Brahmins, Thakurs against Jats, Gujjars versus Ahirs and Mallahs, and so on. These clashes slowly developed into full-fledged robberies, their only means to survive. Kings, emperors, and even British rulers could not stop them. The main reason behind this was the topography of *beehed*. The dacoits were familiar with the lanes and routes of this region, but the troops sent by either British rulers or the Delhi Emperor were unfamiliar to the topography. Even if a battalion of five thousand soldiers got lost in the maze of *beehed*, no one would ever come to know of it.

Even now, life is extremely difficult here. Neither horses

nor vehicles can move in these terrains. I was once lost in this naturally created maze of the *beehed.* For almost an hour I kept fumbling for a way out, and was driven tired and thirsty during the time. But it is not time yet for that tale. It might surprise the readers to know that Abul Fazl, the author of *Ain-i-Akbari*, the Grand Vizier of Akbar, was murdered in these regions. He went against Shehzada Salim, and informed Akbar that Salim was unfit for the throne. Hence Salim planned to get him out of his way. Salim spread rumours among Rajputs that Abul Fazl was trying to convert Hindus. Salim especially provoked his close friend, the then Rajput ruler of Bundelkhand, Raja Vir Singh Bundela, who assassinated Abul Fazl at a place near Narwar in 1603. His grave still lies forlorn in the Antari village in Madhya Pradesh.

Another traveller Huen Tsang remains a testimony to the long history of dacoits in Chambal. And, this Chinese tourist too was not spared by them. For most people, Chambal's history is limited to Mansingh, Malkhan Singh, Phoolan Devi, and a few contemporary popular dacoits. But history proves that Chambal's propensity towards looting and robbery existed since ancient times. Huen Tsang shows how old the terror of Chambal dacoit is. Chinese traveller, Huen Tsang came to India during the reign of Harshavardhan. In 629 AD, at the age of 29 years, he started his journey. Travelling through Tashkand and Samarkand, he reached Gandhar in 630 AD. From there he travelled to Kashmir, Punjab, Kapilavastu, Benaras, Gaya, and Kushinagar. In the seventh century, during Harshavardhan's reign, these dacoits had abducted him near Murena-Dhaulpur and robbed him of his belongings. Huen Tsang was travelling from Harshavardhan's Kannauj to Malwa along the rivers Ganga and Chambal. While travelling by boat, he was suddenly intercepted by the dacoits at the *beehed* near Dhaulpur in Rajasthan. The dacoits had left him only with his books. This episode finds a place even in the writings of Huen Tsang. His foreign attire had made him a target for these dacoits who took him forcefully to a temple in a forest. But as they were preparing to sacrifice him to their goddess, there was a strong dust storm. Scared that the storm was a result of the goddess' ire, the robbers let Huen Tsang go. (Two books, *Oriental Memories: A Narrative of Seventeen Years in Residence in India*, 1834, by James Forbes, and *Thugi*: *Banditry and the British in Early Nineteenth Century India* by Kim A Wagoner, mention this incident. Apart from these, the incident is also recorded in *Imperial Gazeteer of India*, Volume I, second edition.)

PROBLEMS OF *BEEHED*

Before the story of the dacoits or the *baghis* of Chambal, it is important to take a look at the geographical, historical, and economic situation of the place along with its overall environment. It is important to understand how much the natural environment of Chambal is responsible for turning these common people into *baghis*. The origin of uneven terrain and its effect on the economy of the place is also important. Without discussing the above concerns, it will be difficult to understand why people of Chambal leave everything including their families, and plunge into a life of *baghi* in the *beehed*. Before narrating the story of human robbers let us take a look at the extent to which nature has robbed Chambal.

Soil erosion is presently one of the major global problems. The valley or the *ghaati*, as it is known in Bundelkhandi or colloquial Hindi, is formed due to excessive soil erosion that leads to the creation of a very segregated land. The valley is formed due to the rapid flow of the river which is a natural phenomenon. Rivers are one of the most important reasons for soil erosion in India. Every year almost 3.61 crore hectare of land gets displaced due to flowing water. The places most affected by soil erosion are Gujarat, Madhya Pradesh, Rajasthan, and Uttar Pradesh. In the central part of India, the

Chambal Valley is one of the most affected areas of the country and consists of the eroded regions of Madhya Pradesh, Rajasthan, and Uttar Pradesh. Chambal is an important tributary of Yamuna. Locally known as *beehed*, the Chambal Valley has one of the worst soil qualities in India. Several major canals and valleys have come together in the Chambal region. The place lacks development, and has a high crime rate. Around 4800 square kilometre area falls under the *beehed* region, it occupies both the banks of River Chambal. This is the lifeline of this region. The valleys of Chambal are very close to each other and about five to six kilometres of its area are covered by deep canals. Many small and big canals ultimately join the river. This leads to gully formation.

The river is of utmost importance in this region. There is a complex socio-economic structure in the areas of human habitation. More than 80 percent of the people residing in the villages are dependent on farming. There is no major industry in this region, so there are very few alternative sources of livelihood for locals. Soil erosion and gully formation considerably reduce the area of arable land. Farmers of this region have tried to look for solutions regarding the loss of arable land. Some of the practices they follow are building dikes, channelling, changing the routes of canals, alternative modes of growing crops, and most importantly, to try and even their land. There has been an increase in the rate of levelling of uneven land due to the availability of state-sponsored modern machines. But during my tour around the valleys of Chambal, farmers have expressed their woe at the quality of levelled land and its productivity. One of the farmers, who had once taken up huge loans to flatten his land using the machine told me that this method considerably reduced the productivity of the land and that it was a very expensive affair to keep the land even. Except for a few affluent farmers, most of them here have to depend on rains for irrigation. Only some villages have a pump set to draw water. Well-irrigated and levelled land proves to be more productive and profitable during early rains. But immediately after, levelled areas start losing more soil due to erosion. Small holes and gullies come up in the land. And it becomes difficult to maintain these lands. Such lands require continuous levelling and building of small dikes to keep them protected. It is now known that in the past four decades (between 1970-2014), around 600 square kilometres of land has been levelled in the lower region of Chambal Valley. The cost of levelling soil in this way is about Rs 800 per hour. The land chosen for levelling depends on the nearness of location and ease of access. But such unscientific levelling increases the expense of land maintenance. The *beehed* is a part of the collective ecosystem. Levelling of land not only disturbs the ecosystem but also loosens the topsoil which in turn increases possibilities of soil erosion. Such land become more prone to gully formation. It takes almost a year to level the mounds of soil and make the land even. In those years when there is irregular rainfall, the situation deteriorates rapidly because untimely rain leads to major soil erosion in these areas. Gully formation becomes more prominent. Lack of proper and timely care leads to erosion of even virgin land.

Land levelling also influences the socio-economic disparity of this region. Only those who have a substantial amount of wealth and labour can afford to get land levelled and sustain it for cultivation. The entire process needs to be repeated after every rain. A large part of this valley is levelled every year which reduces both forest area as well as cultivable land or land required for animal rearing. This leads to an increase in private ownership of land. Though small farmers level their lands, it is the affluent ones who reap the maximum rewards.

While travelling in this region, I have also seen the multiple ways in which local people make use of the *beehed* in everyday life. It is the primary source of firewood for inhabitants of this place. Babla, Parbati, and Ker or Keriya, which are kinds of thorny plants, bear small fruits twice a year, but they chiefly provide firewood. Wild berries like tenti and ber are used to make pickles, which are then used either for self-consumption, or are sold at the local market. The residents of this area also use the upper region of the *ghaati* or valley for cattle rearing. These areas of shared or common usage get converted to private land when individuals acquire such land areas, level them, and use them for farming.

Other villagers, particularly those of socially backward classes, are prohibited from trespassing these private lands. During my travel around the region, I came across many landless people. They told me that they could not depend anymore on the *beehed* for cattle-grazing like the earlier times because pastures were not easily available. This is also a factor that led to the reduction of the number of milch cattle in this region. Moreover, the ecological interdependence between rain-fed agriculture and farm animals has been disrupted. Many landless farm labourers or poor farmers have been forced to migrate to cities in search of jobs as factory workers, domestic helps, or daily labourers. This usurping of the *beehed* by affluent and powerful people have affected lives of the poor in various ways.

Women of these areas complain about the health-related problems that arise from burning grasses and leaves instead of firewood. According to them, when grasses and leaves are burnt within the house, there is more smoke produced compared to burning firewood. This adversely affects the health of children as well. But in the past few years, it has become difficult to procure firewood, hence it has become a practice to burn leaves and other such things, especially among economically poorer families. This has further deepened the economic divide and pushed this society with an already long history of crimes, towards greater social inequality.

On the other hand, with the destruction of natural habitats, wild animals have started entering farmlands to forage for food. This leads to the destruction of crops. Many farmers have narrated their woe to me for their inability to protect their farms from wild beasts. Many farmers have stopped producing the pulse called *arhar* as it requires more time and hence requires greater security. At times they are also forced to leave their land untilled, unable to find a solution to this problem. Availability of cutting-edge technology and improved means of communication are leading to an even rapid levelling of land in this area.

To local affluent people, lending such machines have become a lucrative way of earning money. There is also a plan to procure unused land for industries. But it is important to test the ecological viability of such projects before embarking upon them in such an ecologically sensitive area. It might not be a good idea to embark upon projects related to the industry, dairy, etc in these regions. According to the topology, geographic activities are still going on in this region, making the region unstable. The area is still going through a phase of geological erosion. There should be a well-planned, sensitive and scientific approach towards conservation and progress in this area to reduce the amount of soil erosion. Any other developmental activity will cause harm to the soil and also increase the amount of sediment deposition in the river bed. This would affect the river ecology and also increase chances of flood in the recent future. The immediate profit derived from levelling of land may lead to greater and irrevocable damage to the system. Hence it is better to prevent this damage from the beginning. Such activities in the *beehed* would not only affect the ecology but also hurt the social structure of the region. And this would cause further migration of the economically backward people of this region. It is important to maintain a holistic approach towards such sensitive ecology. It will not be wise to think only of financial profits in a place like Chambal because money cannot measure the price of nature.

In the last eight years, there has been a 45 percent increase in the *beehed* region in Chambal. This *beehed* has caused around 1,043 villages from Murena, Seopur, and Bhind districts of Madhya Pradesh to be lost forever. The rate at which *beehed* is increasing, it is estimated that by 2050, 55,000 hectares of arable land and around 2,000 villages will be lost to the *beehed*. Rehabilitation of affected people will then become a major challenge for the government. There was a time when the *beehed* was known for its dacoits but now the *beehed* itself is a problem for Chambal. For once, let us take a look and see how much of the region around Chambal and its tributaries have been swallowed up by the *beehed*. Of the 3,000 square kilometres of the Chambal river basin, about 80,000 hectares are now *beehed*. River Kunwari has about 75,000 hectares of the *beehed*. It is 2,036 hectares for River Asan, 1,100 hectares for River Shipra, around 1,000 hectares for Besali, 8,072 hectares for the Kuno, 700 hectares for River Parvati. 2,122 hectares for Sank, and 2,032 for Sindh river. The *beehed* has eaten up 520 villages from Murena district, 173 from Bhind, and 347 from Sheopur.

In 1971 the central home ministry had set up a developmental plan for the *beehed*. According to this plan, Rs 1,224 crore was allocated for 27 years. The plan was to be implemented in four stages of seven years each. But this plan was never implemented. All the three states were proposed to be taken together, and the provision would be made for 55,000 hectares of farming land, 27,000 hectares of horticultural land. Furthermore, 27,500 hectares of land was to increase forest area and used for rearing animals. It was also proposed that in the higher *beehed* region, 2 lakh 20 thousand hectares of land was to be used for water conservation. Channels were to be built to drain out surplus water, and a dam was to be built to save farming land from going to waste. This project was supposed to cost Rs 283.62 crores. In 1977-78, the Madhya Pradesh government had sent this proposed plan to the central government for the development of the *beehed* region. This plan also sought to improve around 1 lakh hectares of land in the districts of Bhind, Murena, Datiya, Gwalior, and Chatarpur of Madhya Pradesh, and make them fit for farming. But even that could not be done. In contemporary Chambal, the number of dacoits in *beehed* is dwindling, but *beehed* itself is engulfing more and more land areas. This is worrisome for both the state and the central governments. Just in Madhya Pradesh as of now around 7,50,000 hectare of land has turned into *beehed*.

Apart from *beehed*, Chambal has another very old problem. That is the problem of caste. *Beehed*, water scarcity, caste issues, and lack of development have made things difficult for Chambal. When I went to Chambal in 2017, I realised that from the outside it looked beautiful and quite developed. But the more I entered the region, I saw the extent of social discrimination and economic problems the locals face. Uttar Pradesh has a few villages where there are permanent houses and concrete roads built under the Prime Minister Housing Scheme, but the condition of Madhya Pradesh is worse. Though there are roadways in the city, villages completely lack them. When I was travelling from Bhind to the village of Bhilai in search of Malkhan Singh, I had two encounters with two Dalit women there which made me realise the extent to which casteism existed there.

Following the trails of the *baghis* when I travelled from village to village, I found the such stories everywhere. Casteism is so deeply rooted in Chambal that Mohar Singh and many other *baghis* did not accept Phoolan Devi as a *baghi* because of her caste. Mohar Singh had even said, 'How can she hold a gun, she was a *Mallah*! The Behemai episode was not her doing. It was her *giroh* that did it.' Chambal is indeed almost free of the dacoits now but it has remained as undeveloped as it was before Independence. And if it continues to remain so, it will not be surprising if once more the dacoits return. In Chambal, dacoits were born out of protest against injustice and caste prejudices. If a solution to it is not found immediately, once again people may hear gunshots ringing loud, once again someone may leave his house and jump into the *beehed*. While travelling in Chambal, I reached the conclusion that though it appears calm from a distance, there is still a simmering fire within.

THE KING OF CHAMBAL

On 3 March 1939, a tall, robust and handsome man stepped out of the iron gate of the Agra jail. He looked around for a while and then started walking. He walked for 80 kilometres till the next evening to reach a small village, Khera Rathor, in the interiors of Uttar Pradesh. After 11 years, he was standing on the porch of his own house. He had gone to jail when he was just 32. Now, he was a middle-aged man of 43. His wife, Rukmini Devi, came out running to see him, happiness shining upon her face. But that was momentary. Immediately after that, she burst out crying. There were tears in the eyes of the man too. These are not happy tears of being reunited with one's family, but were tears of separation. While in jail he had come to know that his eldest son, Yashvant Singh, had been killed in police firing. He slowly sat down at the foot of the wooden charpoy and broke into sobs while trying to console his wife. But the next moment he was surprised to see so much fire in the eyes of his wife even while she was crying.

Rukmini stood up and spoke with all the hate that she could muster, 'Aren't you ashamed of yourself? Sitting here and crying like a coward? Those whoremongers for whom you were imprisoned for 11 years, the bastard police shot your eldest son like a dog, they are roaming freely in the village with their heads held high. And all you do is sit behind your wife's *pallu* and cry! In the name of your Yashwant, I want to see the death of those bastards'. She threw her bangles to her husband and said, 'Wear these. If you don't have the courage, then wear these and keep weeping in a corner of the house.' Rukmini shouted out in Bundelkhandi. Shaking in anger, the man stood up. He must have wondered, 'How dare she say this! He was after all a true Rajput Rathor! How can he keep sitting like a woman wearing bangles.' Crying his heart out, he exclaimed, 'Never!' He ran inside the house and took out his old gun. Listening to the commotion, his three other sons, Subedar Singh, Tehsildar Singh, Sonbaran Singh, rushed out. In extreme anger, he looked at them and said, 'Come with me. From today onwards it will be blood for blood.' He did not wait a moment after that. Opening the back door of the house, Mansingh Rathod Tomar and his three sons jumped into the *beehed*.

I was standing at that very door from which Mansingh had jumped into the *beehed*. Coincidentally, it was the same date—4 March. Even the time matched. Baghi Samrat had left this house at twilight, just as it was during my visit. What an amazing coincidence! The walls were crumbling. The half-broken window panes were infested by termite. Doors have long been stolen. The whole house was about to fall apart, only a few rooms remained intact. Currently, one of Mansingh Rathod's relatives was living there. Beside the back-door was a cowshed. Cow dung and urine were scattered all across the courtyard. One woman sitting on one side of the courtyard, breast-feeding her baby, tried to shield herself from an outsider like me. And Mahavir Singh stood beside me smoking a bidi, narrating the story of Mansingh as it runs in their family. He was the grandson of Baghi Nawab Singh, the elder brother of the *baghi* king, Mansingh. Stretched before me for miles was the ochre-coloured *beehed* and its foliage of thorny bushes. In the glow of the setting sun, the *beehed* shone like a land of gold. I visualised what Mahavir Singh narrated. It felt like a light and sound show, set in a historical background.

'Why are you so lost in thoughts, *babua*?' Mahavir Singh's words brought me back to the present. I smiled at him and asked for some water. He sent his grandson on that errand and said, 'We do not enter their house or talk to them because that bastard is a gambler and has no respect for women.' I realised that Mahavir was talking about his cousin who now lived in this dilapidated house, once famously known as *Mansingh ka Garhi*. How could I explain to Mahavir what I was feeling at that point! Inside my *jhola* still lay a copy of Tarun Bhaduri's *Abhisapta Chambal* (*Cursed Chambal*). I had read that book long back in childhood and picked it up again on the train, during this journey to Chambal. I was left with a few more pages. As a child, I had also watched the movie of *Abhisapta Chambal*. I was lost in emotions that Chambal evokes in every Bengali reader, or those I felt as a child! How could I explain all these to Mahavir Singh? After drinking water, I returned the glass and started walking downhill with Mahavir's grandson. This house was situated on the top of one of the *beehed*s. Mansingh fondly called it *garhi*. Climbing down from the *beehed*, we found Mahavir Singh sitting on a cemented base beside an abandoned well. Before going to *garhi*, I had seen the well from a distance. It was surrounded by dead thorny bushes. He told me, 'So did you see the *garhi*? Now see this well.'

Mansingh was returning with his gang after conducting a robbery in a village in Attar of Madhya Pradesh, just across River Chambal. It was not very far from the village of Khera Rathod. They stopped near a well close to the *garhi* to drink water and refresh themselves. It was early morning and there were many village women near the well. When they saw Mansingh and his people, they moved away to make space for them. All the members of Mansingh's troop washed and drank water. They had to travel another kilometre before reaching *garhi*. After marching ahead for a while, Mansingh suddenly realised that there was one person less in his group. But that was not how it should have been. He immediately asked his favourite companion, Rupnarayan or Rupa Maharaj, to look into the matter. Rupa pointed towards the well. A look in that direction was enough to make his blood boil. The person missing from his gang was none other than his nephew, Arvind. He was standing near the well and was tugging at the *pallu* of one of the girls there. His anger knew no bounds. He who was revered almost as God throughout Chambal, whom people affectionately called Raja Mansingh, and paid respect due to an elder brother, he who was also the terror in that entire region, had to see one of his gang members and relative dishonour a woman! He was always respectful towards women of his village and considered it a sin to indulge in alcohol and womanising. It was a diktat even within his troop that whatever you do, never insult a woman. And being a member of such a gang, he was behaving like this! Mansingh took a few steps forward. In his worldview, there was no mercy for anyone who insulted a woman. He looked towards Rupa once and in a flash targeted his rifle. Bang! A bullet went through the forehead of Arvind. But not even paying a second glance in that direction, Mansingh turned around and began walking. He was Mansingh, about whom villagers believed that whatever might happen, he would never let a woman be dishonoured. He was the same Mansingh about whom the minstrels sang—

Yahan ki baatein yahan par rah gayi aage
Aur badal gayi jaye
Alha garo Mansingh ke mitron
Sunlo kan lagaye

'This is that well.' Mahavir and I were sitting near that well, surrounded by thorny bushes. Indefatigable, Mahavir kept narrating one story after another from a past that belonged some six or seven decades back. A boy went cycling past us, a big black water container and a few bottles were tied to his cycle. Mahavir shouted out to him. When the boy stopped, Mahavir walked towards him and picked up one of the bottles. After drinking water from one of those, he returned by my side. Mahavir did not visit this place much. He had come here today for me. Instead of drinking water at his relative's house, he asked for it from a roadside stranger because that relative here gambles and does not respect women. So many years ago, his grandfather had shot one of his kin and gang member dead for dishonouring a woman. In similar times, Mahavir might have acted in the same way. Or it might have turned the other way as well, Mahavir might have found himself in the place of the person playing with a woman's honour. In his veins ran the blood of his grandfather, the infamous Nawab Singh, the one who fell into bad company since childhood and there was not any crime left that he did not commit. The police records about him stated 'Nawab Singh learnt nothing lawful in his life. His life was an unrelieved pattern of criminality' (I had read about this in *Abhisapto Chambal* and also found it in the old records of Uttar Pradesh police. To tell you the truth, the amount of documentation on the crimes of Mansingh and his gang that is available in the police record rooms should be enough to build a museum on the dacoits of Chambal. Even later records that I have seen in police stations of Uttar Pradesh and Madhya Pradesh that fall under the Chambal region are things worth seeing).

Absent-mindedly, I lit a cigarette. My mind was in a state of excitement. I was listening to a thrilling but true story that had been first written by a Bengali journalist some 58 years back, a story that I had read as a child. And now, I, as a journalist, was listening to the same story right from the mouth of the grandson of the protagonist. I could feel history unfolding once again before my eyes. It was as if I was watching a black and white film in this age of developing technologies. I was shivering with exhilaration. '*Chal Babua*, I shall now take you to Baba's temple.' Mahavir got up and sat behind his grandson on the bike and asked me to sit behind him. On the left was Mansingh's *garhi*, on the right, a series of *beehed*. The bike moved between these.

My expedition to Chambal started from Agra in Uttar Pradesh but there is a beginning even before that. It started a few more weeks earlier. This was March, 2017. Last month the proprietor of the newspaper I work for, Swapan Kanti Ghosh, told me, 'Subhendu, it has been long since you went out of the city for an assignment. This time I shall give you an interesting subject, something that you will enjoy. You will have to go to Chambal. My next cover story will be on the dacoits of Chambal.' I was surprised. I was new to journalism, only eight months in this profession. Before this I had taken up two assignments away from the city, both were very challenging and I was successful in both. Even then, Chambal and dacoits were something beyond my imagination! My first problem is that the moment I sniff adventure, I cannot remain calm. It was bound to pull me in. And secondly, I have never learnt to decline any assignment. Still, an assignment in Chambal did catch me a bit unaware, and I think our editor, Ekram Ali, could understand that. He had great faith in me and that is why probably, to boost my confidence, he kept on encouraging me. Along with him, there were my colleagues Santu, Sudipto, and of course the poet, Ranjan Bandopadhyay. Ekram da kept saying to these three, 'As soon as I saw Subhendu with a stud in one ear, I knew he had it in him. Do you know Ranjan da, one of the best things about Subhendu is that he never says no! I can vouch for the fact that no one could have accomplished what he did in the project on Benaras. There is nothing to worry about, come now, pass me a cigarette.' Though Ekram da's encouraging words expanded my chest from 32 to 36 inches, the moment

I thought of Chambal, it shrank back to 23. The fact that worried me the most about Chambal was that I had no information or references about the place. When I said this to Ekram, he suggested that I read the books *Abhisapto Chambal* and *Beehed, Baghi, Banduk.* He also asked me to read the article on Chambal written by poet, Mridul Dasgupta, published in *Parivartan*, the magazine.

Mridul Dasgupta had been to Chambal in 1981. When I got in touch with him, he suggested a route, and that I first go to Uttar Pradesh and from there to Madhya Pradesh, and then again from there to Rajasthan via Uttar Pradesh, finally entering Madhya Pradesh. Moreover, he had been there in 1981 so he could not even name any place that might help me in the search. He told me that during his trip, he managed to get references after a lot of effort, which finally helped him gain entry into villages or establish contact with dacoits. He said in clear terms that going there without any reference will not be of any use at all, 'No one will entertain your queries.' But he also told me that I could begin my quest from the open-air jail in Jalaon village which had been built particularly for the dacoits. Extensive searches on the internet did not yield anything more than a few myths about the dacoits. Even Tarun Bhaduri's works had just a few names of villages and dacoits, but no other information. Still, I started with my research with those two books as primary texts. Of course, along with that was Ekram da's incessant pep talk—'You are the only one who can do it.' I realised that I had dug my own grave. But today I have no qualms in accepting that without the constant encouragement of Ekram da and Ranjan da, I could not have reached this place. So started my independent research on Chambal. But Chambal did not mean a single place. Chambal meant three largest states of India and thousands of villages in these three states. From where was I supposed to start my search for the dacoits? The only information that I had was names of few villages, and names of some extremely dangerous dacoits. I did not even know whether those villages existed anymore, or whether the dacoits whose names I have had in hand were alive. With fate as my only companion, I ventured on my journey. On 2 March 2017, I boarded the Ananya Express to reach Agra. There were several benefits of going to Agra. Firstly, there was an excellent bus service between Agra and other areas of Uttar Pradesh and Madhya Pradesh. Secondly, I was more familiar with Agra than any other place in Uttar Pradesh. Also, since I had been in Delhi for a considerable period, I had many acquaintances in Rajasthan and Uttar Pradesh. If need be, I knew I could get help from them.

I reached Agra on 3 March, at three in the afternoon. The train was delayed by five hours. This was that same 3 March when 39 years back Mansingh had stepped out of his prison in Agra after serving his term and had walked towards his village. He had reached his village the next day, on 4 March. And on that very day, he had taken his rifle and jumped into the *beehed* to become Baghi Samrat. Coincidentally, I too was supposed to reach his village on the same date and reach that door from where he along with his sons had escaped into the unknown and strange life of the *beehed*. With much difficulty, I managed to find a place in a hotel. It was close to the Taj Mahal, even though visiting that place was not my intention. Agra has two inter-state bus terminals—Idgah and Bijlighar. Bijlighar had a greater number of buses going to Khera Rathod. And it being near to Taj Mahal, I thought I shall be able to kill two birds with one stone. But it was my misfortune that as I walked through Mughal Garden to reach Taj Mahal, I found it closed, the day being a Friday. Hence, I concentrated on other tasks at hand. I saw some policemen patrolling the area. I sat on a bench close by and engaged them in a light conversation. From them, I learnt that the best route would be to take a bus from Bijlighar to Jaitpur Kalan in the Bah district and then another bus from there to Khera Rathod. I also gathered some important information regarding Chambal. Due to tiredness, I woke up late the next day. I hurriedly freshened up, paid the hotel bill and checked out with my luggage. My luggage consisted of a single rucksack. Initially, I had thought of making Agra my base. But then I realised that I neither had a route map nor much information. I did not know which way I would have to go. Hence it was better to carry all my things along. I decided that I shall proceed as per information gathered in the course of my journey. In a way, it meant that the flow of events would determine my route. Around eleven in the morning I boarded a bus belonging to Uttar Pradesh state road transport from Bijlighar bus stand. My destination was Jyotpur Kalan in the Bah district. Before boarding the bus, I had a breakfast of *puri sabzi* from one of the shops at the bus stand. The lesser said about the bus journey, the better.

The distance between Agra and Jyotpur Kalan was about 90-95 kilometres. In this route, each time the bus stopped, the bus would get a little more crowded with villagers and their livestock such as goats, poultry animals, etc. Their calls along with abuses hurled by the passengers made it a hell of a journey. But I must also say that this torturous journey turned out to be a blessing in disguise. Before leaving, Ekram da had repeatedly warned me not to reveal my identity as a journalist unless I was in grave danger. But I did just the opposite. It is in my nature to do exactly the opposite of what I am asked to do. Moreover, from my previous experience in Uttar Pradesh and Bihar, I knew the significance that villagers attached to the word *patrakar* or journalist, and how much they both feared and revered those who came under this category. Therefore, during conversations, I deliberately revealed my identity to people. So, I just spread the word that I was a journalist from Kolkata, here to do a feature on the dacoits of Chambal. Luckily this plan turned out to be brilliant. Many people gave me information on their own.

When Tarun Bhaduri visited Chambal, that was the best time for the dacoits. Though the media was not very strong during those times, he did not have any problem in finding *baghis*. Also, as a member of a well-known newspaper house, he carried a lot more influence. On the other hand, I was new to journalism, and by the time I visited Chambal, most of the dacoits had surrendered themselves and vanished. Many of them had returned to social life, and were staying in cities for their security. With only a handful of names, I did not know where to start. I believed only these villagers could be of help to me. I gave in to my impulse and it yielded result. From internet searches, I found that Khera Rathod was Mansingh's village. So, I thought of going there first.

During this long journey by bus, I befriended the conductor and got some important information from him. Conductor Rajbir Kushawa informed me that the word *baghi* was almost extinct in Chambal and the word 'dacoit' was taking its place because today's dacoits were not as principled as their predecessors. They did not become robbers due to any social injustice, rather, have chosen the path voluntarily. I kept listening to him even though I felt quite restless, because acquiring information on the current situation of Chambal was not my only agenda. Of course, it was important to know that, but I also needed addresses of those dacoits whose names I had—Mansingh, Malkhan Singh, Mohar Singh, Rupnarayan Singh or Rupa Maharaj, Tehsildar Singh, Lokman Dixit or Lukka Dacoit, Laxman Singh, Gabbar Singh, Sultana dacoit, Putlibai, Seema Parihar, Kusuma Nain and many others. I kept fidgeting. The bus had stopped at a stop on Lucknow Express-way for a tea break.

When it was on the move again, the bus was quite crowded. I felt as if I was travelling by goods train. I regretted my decision to travel by such a ramshackle government bus to save money instead of taking a private one. But after a while, the journey paid back. A villager from one of the seats in the back came to me with folded hands and pleaded, '*Babua*, my daughter is pregnant. Could you please give her the window seat? She is not feeling well and may throw up.' I gave my seat to that girl and went to sit beside the old man. 'Thank you so much *sahib*, where are you going? You do not seem to belong to this place.' Was it written on my face that I was a Bengali, I wondered. I replied, '*Baba*, I am a journalist. I have come here to know about the *baghis* of Chambal.' The old man said, '*Arre* Ram Ram! Where will you find any *baghi* now? They used to be here once upon a time, not anymore. Nowadays you may find a few robbers in Chambal, but they are not *baghis*.' What did the old man mean? The land of dacoits was without dacoit now! I asked him once again, 'Then what should I do? I want to go to Mansingh's house in Khera Rathod.' He told me that to go to Khera Rathod, I should get down at Jyot Kalan and take a jeep from there. It was an hour from there. In that long journey, I came across a lot of information from that old man. He told me that though the government has made proper roads here, it still lacks conveyance.

All through the day, just a few buses were plying to and from Agra. There has not been much progress in people's lifestyle. Whatever developments have taken place, they have only been in the city. It was a two-hour journey. Along the way, I could see some reputed private schools in the villages beside SH60 Lucknow Expressway. I don't know why, but these schools seemed more like a visual pain to me. The condition of villages, the kind of people, their social status, that I could make out during this journey, clearly indicated that these schools were not for the villagers. All these schools were for people higher up the social ladder. When I mentioned this to the old man, he pointed his hands upwards and said, '*Betua*, from where shall we have the means to send our children to these schools! The city boys and girls come here to study. These are American schools. For our kids, we have those government schools.' He pointed towards a few houses with thatched roofs. I realised that over the ages Chambal hasn't undergone any change in terms of class discrimination. Or perhaps there have been some changes, perhaps these hard-working people have started earning more than before but that hasn't brought them the affluence that is required to put their wards in English medium schools. Though we have been travelling together for a long time, I still did not know my companion's name. On asking he said he was Mohan Singh, a farmer by profession. He lived near Jot Kalyan. I asked him whether he had ever seen a dacoit. He said, 'Yes *beta*, I have seen a lot of them. But they were *baghis*, not dacoits. Dacoits are brutal and unprincipled. But Chambal used to have *baghis*—they were ruthless but not cruel and had very strong values. They never looted the poor. They were against crimes and injustice by *zamindars*.' I asked him if he had seen Mansingh to which he replied, 'No I never got a chance to see him but have heard a lot about him from my father and grandfather. I have seen Rupa Maharaj, Mansingh's right-hand person, and his son Tehsildar Singh. I had seen Mansingh after his death when the police had kept his corpse on the ground at Gwalior for people to see. The whole village had turned out to see him for the last time. No one could believe that our *dau* was no more!' I was reminded of *Abhisopto Chambal* where Tarun Bhaduri had mentioned that in those days people of central India used to believe that there did not exist a bullet that could kill Mansingh. The author had also described the death of Mansingh in these words—'The next morning Mansingh's body was kept on the ground in Kumpu in Gwalior for people to see and satisfy their curiosity. Mansingh was tied on a charpoy with tight ropes. Beside him was the corpse of his son, Subedar Singh. A board was kept near them that stated—Killed by special armed police at Kakaran-ka-Pura, Bhind: 25-08-55: Dacoits, Mansingh and Subedar Singh.' This old man here was present that day in the crowd of people who had turned up to see Mansingh. Like many others, perhaps he too had believed that such a bullet that could kill Mansingh did not exist. The bus journey came to an end. Reaching Jyot Kalan, I got off the bus.

Jyotpur Kalan! I was completely bewildered after getting off the bus. Which way should I proceed! The place where I had got off the bus was not a proper bus stop. It was a market area in a small village. I craved some tea and was hungry too. The *puri sabzi* that I had had in the morning was all digested in the bumpy bus ride. I walked a bit and entered a tea shop. I felt no attraction for any of the food that was available in the other shops around that place. They only had fried snacks like *kachori,* or *samosa,* or bread *pakoda*. A couple of sweet shops were there too, but after some deliberations, I preferred tea. This is one thing that is common all over India—a tea joint will not only stave off your hunger but may also help you with your work. This is a place where people from various classes come together and due to a heterogeneous gathering of people, one may even come across valuable information. It is a phenomenon that I have found common in many states like Delhi, Uttar Pradesh, West Bengal, Punjab, Haryana, and states in Southern India. We Bengalis have a notion that we are the only ones who while away time in tea joints, but that is not true. It holds true for the entire country. Here a Punjabi businessman can converse for hours with a cobbler on topics ranging from politics to cricket. In fact, in Delhi, I have seen deals worth crores of rupees being finalised in these places. I have also seen *supari* killers being given their contracts in such tea joints. I had all these in mind when I decided to enter the tea stall. Since it was afternoon, it was less crowded. People will start coming again from around 3 pm. The few that were there in the stall were mostly villagers. A boy came and took the order for tea. Since I was looking here and there, the stall owner asked, '*Saab*, do you need anything more? Are you searching for something?' I asked him for some biscuits with the tea and then enquired about the route to Khera Rathod. I also asked about lodging facilities available there. The old tea stall owner told me the direction to the jeep stand. He said that these jeeps will take me to Khera Rathod.

After finishing the tea, I paid my bills, picked up my rucksack, and walked towards the jeep stand. On both sides of the almost-broken road, there were a few permanent shops. In front of one of the closed shops was an ancient open-hooded jeep. Inside, a few village men and women were sitting. Somehow, I managed a seat in one corner. But after waiting for around 15 minutes, I was too impatient to remain seated and got down. Lighting a cigarette, I irritably asked the driver, 'At what time will it start?' He replied with a complete nonchalance that the jeep will move only when it was full. Till then there had been just 8-10 passengers and according to the driver's words, the jeep will start moving only when there will be around 30-35 people sitting inside, on footholds on either side, upon the bonnet, etc. What was the man saying! A broken road, such a dilapidated jeep, and 30-35 passengers! On seeing my amazement, the driver asked me about my destination. When I said it was Khera Rathod, he further enquired whose house I wanted to visit. I replied, 'house of Mansingh, the *baghi*.' He measured me from head to toe and said, 'But he has passed away long back. That's *dau*'s grandson over there. Go and meet him, he will take you to his home. He is also waiting for this jeep.' Mansingh's grandson! I turned around to see and was taken aback. How could this person be Mansingh's grandson? I had always associated the word dacoit with a sturdy body, big moustache, and a fierce appearance. Yet what I saw was an old man, almost bent down upon the road, hardly 5'4" in height, with a sparse moustache, and having frequent bouts of heavy coughs. The driver shouted out to him, 'O Mahavir! Here is someone looking for Mansingh-ji. Take him to your place.' I was quite disappointed. I had come to work with dacoits, not with a dirty weakling like him. Hesitantly I approached the man squatting in front of the closed door. On seeing me, Mahavir or Mahavir Singh Rathod shouted in a true Bundelkhandi voice, 'Where have you come from? What do you do? Who are you?' I was already put off by his appearance. To add to it, he was questioning me as if I was a subject of interrogation in a king's court. But I was the one in need. I was a stranger here, and yet I have received a golden opportunity. Fussing too much about my hurt ego wouldn't help me at all. So, I said, '*Chacha*, I am a journalist from Kolkata. I have come here to know more about Mansingh.'

'You want to know about Baba? Then come to my place, I shall introduce you to everyone.' I offered him a cigarette in the hope of improving the new relationship, but he refused my offer saying that cigarettes were bland and made him cough more. Bidis were better, he said. By this time, there was no place left inside the jeep. Mahavir said, 'I shall sit on the bonnet, you too come and sit with me.' I took my rucksack and went to sit beside Mahavir. On the way, I asked him if there was any place to stay at Khera Rathod and also whether I could return today itself after my work was over. He asked me not to worry saying both the options were available. I could stay or return as I wish. By then the surrounding had started changing. As the jeep progressed along the bumpy road, I could see houses on either side. Some had thatched roofs, some were mud houses, but very few concrete houses. We could see barley, paddy and maize fields, and much more. After a while, Mahavir started talking about himself in a hushed voice. As many times I enquired him regarding a place to stay, he kept nodding in affirmative. For some reason, I was not assured by his replies. There were so few vehicles on road. There were no buses, I could only see tractors or motorbikes. By then, Mahavir had changed his way of addressing from the formal '*aap*' to the informal '*tu.*' He went on talking, 'Why don't you stay with me? I shall lay the *charpoy* for you. Once you finish talking to everyone, you can lie down to sleep.' I realised that there was no accommodation available in Khera Rathod and considering the time, it would also not be possible to return from there the same day. As soon as I informed this development to Ekram da, he was extremely excited. He kept saying over the phone, 'Do not leave him, try and get even the smallest details from him. Go and see how a dacoit's house looks.' Suddenly, to my amazement, the jeep got off the road and started moving through paddy fields. It went and stopped in front of a house. After a while, four women got down and the jeep stuttered back on the road. In this way, the jeep kept on dropping off passengers at their doorsteps. Mahavir kept up his steady stream of monologue about himself—that he did not care about anyone, that he worked in the forest department but attended office only when it suited his whims. Mostly he just went twice a month—once at the beginning and then again to collect his salary. He said that all officers were scared of him, but he wasn't bothered with any of them, that he was his own master. The only thing I could do was to keep nodding to Mahavir's words. I left myself to fate. I wished to see what Khera Rathod had in store for me. If it came to worse, I could spend one night anywhere. After more than an hour's travelling, the jeep reached Khera Rathod. Getting off the jeep, Mahavir took me along the cemented road, continuing his monologue. The faster I walked, the slower was Mahavir's pace. Several times there were such heavy bouts of coughing that I became apprehensive of him reaching home safely. But whoever went along the road, he stopped to talk to them, and after every person, he would tell me, 'Everyone respects me here.' I kept nodding obediently. What else could I have done!

After walking for about one and a half kilometres, we reached Mahavir's house. It was Mahavir's house and not Mansingh's. It was partly made of bricks and partly mud. On one side was an open veranda. There was a large courtyard. There was a temporary shed for cattle on the left side. Just beyond the courtyard was the muddy track, the one we had to take to reach the house. Beyond that was the *beehed.* There was a potato farm in front of the house. The houses in the village were separated from each other by almost a kilometre and a half which meant that even if I was murdered, no one will come to know of it. As soon as we entered the house, Mahavir loudly called out to his family. Then he laid down the iron charpoy. But after that, the fun began. That Mahavir who was making such tall claims a moment ago suddenly retreated into a shell. His wife, a middle-aged woman with a larger *ghunghta* drawn over her face, came out. She snubbed him into silence for not informing her beforehand about the guest at home. Then she turned towards me with folded hands and said, 'Please don't mind *babuji*, he is always so irresponsible.' By then the grandchildren had surrounded Mahavir. Mahavir had two sons. The younger one ran a dairy farm while the other was a farmer. Four or five children were in the house, belonging to both his sons. The eldest granddaughter was going to take her grade 10 board exam that year and the next one was in the ninth grade. The others were in school too. Mahabir laid down the charpoy under the bael tree in the courtyard and said that the two of us will sleep there. Tea with *namkeens* and mixtures arrived. Once tea was over, Mahavir asked his grandson to take out his bike. Here, the modes of conveyance were restricted to personal bikes, bicycles or tractors. Or you could just stand on the road and wait for a lift. Two government buses ran in the morning and for the rest of the day, there were a few jeeps. There was no power supply for the greater part of the day which made batteries an indispensable part of their lives.

Mahavir's wife kept muttering under her breath throughout the period. Mahavir tried to scold her once—'Why don't you take care of our guest?' He asked his younger son to kill a goat for the occasion and to bring foreign liquor for me. I kept on insisting that all these were not required, but Mahavir turned a deaf ear. Finally, his wife lost patience and said, 'Keep calm, I shall do all these. You need not advise. Go and sit over there.' Mahavir made a long face and went to sit on the charpoy. The scene was quite amusing and I found it difficult to retain a serious face. A successor of such a mighty *baghi* too was scared of his wife! And here I was thinking that only I belonged to that lot. By then, Mahavir's wife had taken my rucksack inside the house and the children were fiddling with my camera and phone. Over another cup of tea with Mahavir, the actual story started unfolding. Mansingh, Nawab Singh, Tehsildar Singh—all were dead. But their descendants are staying in this village only in separate houses. Mansingh's *garhi* was further down the road, behind this house.

As I was drinking tea, I saw Mahavir's son slaughtering a big goat near their cattle shed. After some time, in between narrating stories, Mahavir proposed going to the *garhi*. We rode his bike to go to Mansingh's old fort. We took the road that was just behind the house. On either side, there were huge mounds of soil and thorny bushes, a straight concrete road ran in between. Wind was blowing and it seemed the *beehed* was secretly beckoning us. It was an unsettling feeling. But Mahavir was inured to these. He kept instructing his grandson regarding changing gears and chided whenever the young boy would speed up. After approximately three kilometres, we stopped at a place from where Mahavir pointed at an upward incline and said, 'Baba's *garhi* is over there.' He asked his grandson to take me there and he himself sat upon a mound. Ruins of a fort-like structure lay between the forest and the *beehed*. Only a few rooms were still intact. This was the impenetrable *garhi* that the Robinhood of Chambal, Dau Mansingh had built. After his death, police had taken over the place. It was in this *garhi* that Rukmini Devi, Mansingh's wife had narrated his story to the young Tarun Bhaduri. Here, only the then Home Minister, Kailashnath Katju, had come with a request for Mansingh's surrender. And it was from this place that Mansingh along with his elder brother and three sons had jumped into the *beehed* to avenge the killing of his eldest son. This *garhi* was very close to Mansingh's heart, it was his palace, his *durbar*. But who was this Mansingh? Why did he become a *baghi*? Most of us do not know why those who are referred to as dacoits by rest of India, considered themselves *baghis*. *Baghi*—the word meant rebel. They were those who revolted against the atrocities of rich zamindars, police, and administrators, and jumped into the *beehed*. They were the ones who were called *baghis*. They sacrificed themselves to the age-old tradition of Chambal—*Khoon ke badle khoon* or blood for blood. The history of Chambal carries pieces of evidence of this baying for blood. Children of Chambal grow up listening to *alhas*, the songs that celebrate the bravery of the ancient heroes of that place—Alha and Udal.

Barah baras lou kukur jeebe
Baki to fir jeebe siyaar
Jaaki bairi jeebit baitha
Uyake jeeban rahe dhikkar

(Or, it is only for 12 years that a fighter lives, rest of his life is that of a fox. The one whose enemy still exists lives a life equivalent to hell.)

This is the chief mantra of Chambal, or the ancient precept of an eye for an eye. Let us return to the question we began with—who was Mansingh? Why did he become a *baghi*, the terror of Chambal, its unrivalled king, Dau Mansingh Rathod?

Mansingh was born in 1896 as the second son of Bihari Singh, a trader in the village of Khera Rathod. Immediately after his birth, the village astrologer had declared that he will grow up to be a great man. His father lovingly named him Mansingh in remembrance of the great Rajput king. From an early age Mansingh or Manua, as his father called him affectionately, was the leader of the village boys. He had a gang of his own, of boys who unquestionably accepted his authority. Mansingh kept himself fit and healthy through regular work-out. His father traded in stolen goods. In the dead of the night, gangs of dacoits would come to his house to sell their stolen goods. He owned five bighas of land in the village, but how much could one earn from that! Being a Rajput, Bihari wanted fame, honour, and respect like that commanded by the affluent Brahmins or Thakurs. Thus began his nightly transactions and lending practice. In a short while, he became the Shylock of the village, lending money at very high interest. When people could not repay, he took away their properties. Among his clients, was a man called Bhola Singh who could not repay the money and Bihari Singh was determined to take away all that the poor man had. He kept on trying to acquire the small house owned by Bhola Singh. So Bhola sought help from another rich Brahmin within the village, Purohit Talfiram, who already had a bitter relationship with Bihari. Both of them were contenders for the post of the village headman and that caused deep resentment between them. So Talfiram advised Bhola Singh to go to court and not pay a single paisa to Bihari. Both the sides got engaged in a fight and the entire village quaked with fear. Bihari Singh told his younger son, 'How can you stay quiet in spite of being a Rajput?'

After this, Mansingh developed a friendship with the police. He got licenses for firearms both for himself and for his elder brother, Nawab Singh. Talfiram got scared. Immediately after that, there was a robbery in the adjacent village called Mahua. Talfiram implicated Mansingh in the crime but the police could not find any evidence against him. Talfiram then suggested Chidda Singh, the person whose house had been robbed, to file a case against Mansingh. Now it was Mansingh's turn to be scared. He offered an out-of-court settlement with Chidda. Chidda Singh, emboldened by the support and money of Talfiram, not only refused the offer but also sent Mansingh away after insulting him. He clearly stated that he would follow Talfiram's advice and now they would see each other in court. He further suggested that if Mansingh wanted to arrive at any kind of compromise, he must go to Talfiram. Mansingh got furious. On his way to court, Mansingh and his gang attacked Talfiram and Chidda. Even this time police could not get any evidence against Mansingh. On 29 July 1928, Mansingh and his people attacked the house of Shukbasi, a relative of Chidda. Talfiram, on getting the news also rushed there with his gang. There was a bloodbath in the village. But this time, for the first and last time in his life, Mansingh was caught and handcuffed. He was awarded a life sentence and deportation. All the members of his gang were awarded five years imprisonment. Mansingh's elder brother, Nawab Singh, his son, Yashwant Singh, and nephew, Darshan Singh, were on the run. Two of his most trusted men, Kheem Singh and Bhup Singh, went and joined Talfiram's gang. Even in jail, Mansingh received news regarding the hardships that his son, brother, and nephew were facing to stay on the run—lack of food and money forced them to commit petty thefts and robberies. On 5 December 1937, the most dreaded news reached Mansingh—his eldest son, Yashwant Singh, and nephew, Darshan Singh, had been killed in a police encounter. His elder brother was also arrested and given a life sentence. The only companion that Mansingh had in prison was his old and ailing friend, Chabram. His only son, Rupnarayan Sharma or Rupa, used to visit both of them during their period of imprisonment. Chabram's health kept failing and he too died but before dying he made Mansingh promise that the latter would look after Rupa as his own son. Mansingh took an oath in the name of his dead son. Meanwhile, Bihari Singh put in a lot of effort and money to get Mansingh released from prison.

After eleven long years, on 3 March 1939, Mansingh

came out of prison. A few days after, bloodied bodies of Talfiram and his two relatives, Ratiram and Sonapal were found in a field in the village. These two were probably the ones who had informed about the secret hideout of Yashwant and Nawab Singh which ultimately led to the death of Mansingh's elder son. This was Mansingh's revenge. But all these were much before Mansingh's rise as the king of bandits or his reign of terror. This marked Mansingh's initiation into the world of *baghis*. Talfiram's son, Netaram, informed the police. Once again, Mansingh and his sons fled from home. This was the period when Mansingh emerged as a living terror of Chambal. For Talfiram and his family, he personified death. He repeatedly attacked Netaram's house and set fire on his properties. He unleashed his ire upon the wealthy people of Chambal. He attacked such people in various districts and Agra bore the brunt of his *tandava*. The whole of Agra quaked in fear. Finally, Uttar Pradesh police woke up and started Operation Mansingh. But that did not help much. There were a few skirmishes between the gang and the police but mostly Mansingh and his men remained out of bounds. Then in August 1943, Mansingh killed Nawab Singh Gujjar of Sarhai village, suspecting him to be a police spy. The very next year, the two nephews of Netaram, Mewa Ram and Jeth Ram too fell prey to Mansingh's ire, within a gap of few days. Mansingh had promised to himself that he won't leave anyone to carry on the lineage of those who had been involved in the death of his son. So, he kept on murdering Talfiram's family members one after the other. When India became independent on 14th August 1947, Mansingh's elder brother, Nawab Singh was released from jail as well. Immediately after coming out of jail, Nawab Singh chose the path of robbery but not together with Mansingh. On one side was Mansingh and on the other, Nawab Singh. Then suddenly, one fine day, Mansingh returned to Khera Rathod.

By then his father had died and his elder brother was a

fugitive. So, he became the head of the family. He now used the money that he had accumulated from looting and plundering to build a huge and strong fort-like house in place of the old one. Villagers named it *garhi*. Mansingh became quite an influential person in the village. He was everyone's *dau* (leader). In any kind of crisis, to solve any dispute, to arrange dowry for daughter's wedding, they depended on Mansingh. He slowly turned into a modern-day Robinhood of Kheda Rathod and Chambal. Everyone knew that *dau* looted the rich to distribute the wealth among the poor. His hatred was for the rich, the police, and the police spy. But he never killed any policeman or spy unless it was necessary. The situation became such that even government officers of the lower level came to Mansingh with their problems. Some came with gifts for him and some went away with gifts. Mansingh was invited to village weddings and if he failed to attend one, it was the host's loss or misfortune. Mansingh became almost legendary in Chambal, so much so that there were songs written on him and even mothers sang lullabies in his name to put babies to sleep—

Aja re nindiya aja
woh dekh dwar khada Man Singh raja

(Come oh sleep! Come / See, Raja Man Singh stands near the door)

But Mansingh did not forget his son Yashwant's death. So, he organised a grand marriage celebration for Yashwant's son Bharat Singh. People were amazed at the amount of money that was spent on the occasion. Even police records contain the details of that wedding—

'The people were spellbound by the fine spectacle of five grand cars and three majestic elephants gorgeously caparisoned for the marriage procession. It was attended by the gentry far and near...

It appears fantastic but Mansingh indeed celebrated the marriage of his grandson in his village home, in great style. Elephants and several cars were in attendance. The big dinner and dancing party that followed was attended by the *tahsildar*, the local medical officer, and the officer in charge of the police station. Without any exception, the big zamindars and the local *mahajans* or money lenders were either present or were presented.'

But one who is already addicted to robbery cannot enjoy domestic life for long. Even Mansingh could not. So once again Mansingh became a terror for Uttar Pradesh. This time even his elder brother Nawab Singh had joined forces. He became a major cause of concern for high-level officers in the police department. After repeated meetings, they decided that to restore some kind of balance in the village they needed to bring back Talfiram's son, Netaram. So Netaram returned to his village under police protection. A police posting was set up near Mansingh's *garhi*. Even then, Netaram became the target of repeated attacks by Mansingh. Finally, a platoon of police force was deployed near river Chambal, approximately eight kilometres from the *garhi*, to stop Mansingh from escaping. But even then, Mansingh got away. This time he reached Madhya Pradesh. Despite chasing him repeatedly, the police could not lay a finger on Mansingh. Just six months later, four of Netaram's relatives were brutally murdered. And exactly a week later, under the cover of the night, Mansingh murdered Netaram, the last surviving descendent of Talfiram. He picked up the gun and killed a Brahmin for the last time. Thus ended a chapter of Mansingh's life. But that did not put an end to his life as a *baghi*. Other incidents followed—his son's injury in police firing, his subsequent anger on the police and so on. One whole book could be written just on him. But my intention is not to author a book on Mansingh's life. I want to trace the history of Chambal along with its contemporary situation and also record the lives of many other *baghis* who have grown up in the *beehed* of Chambal.

It was almost 6:30 in the evening. Day ends a little late in Uttar Pradesh, than in West Bengal. Sitting near the well, I could see the golden sky of twilight reflecting against the *beehed*; it dazzled my sight. I did not feel like leaving at all. I wished to enter those narrow alleys of the *beehed* and unearth stories of mystery, tragedy, blood, and death trapped in the huge mounds of earth in the *beehed*. But I knew that was not possible. One life will never be enough to unravel the mystery that is the *beehed*. Every turn in this place had stories of a new *baghi*, new life, unknown tragedies, blood, tear, and sweat. As I sat listening to the stories, evening set in. Mahavir Singh hurried, there was another place to visit. Even while returning, Mahavir's instruction to his grandson on the rider's seat continued. Whenever the boy rode a little fast, Mahavir snapped at him. On our way I could see ripened mustard plants in the farms stooping low, potatoes being loaded in the tractors. Mahavir informed me that there had been a good harvest of mustard that year. He also asked whether there were farms in Kolkata too. Then we reached Puran Singh's house. In these villages, houses were not huddled together as found in the villages of Bengal. Here, each house was at a distance of about a kilometre and a half from the other. In between, there were either farms or uneven earthen mounds of saffron *beehed*.

Puran Singh was the only son of Mansingh's fourth son, Sonvaran Singh. He had received a bit of education. He told us that after the death of Mansingh, the government had seized the *garhi* and almost 800 bighas of his land. Tehsildar Singh was still in jail, Sonvaran and Rupa were in charge of the gang. They could finally get back the land, after a lot of hassles in 1959, but by then Sonvaran and Subedar were dead. The government divided the land among the descendants of Mahavir Singh. Each grandchild of Mansingh received around 200 bighas of land. Among these cousins, one was working in the forest department. Another, whose name was G.M. Singh, retired as DIG, BSF and was currently staying in Uttar Pradesh. When Sonvaran Singh died, Puran Singh was just six years old. He had been brought up by his grandmother, Mansingh's wife, Rukmini Devi. Though he told me that all his grandchildren were studying in the village school, he was not too keen to talk much about himself. He said that in Khera Rathod these days, Thakurs and Mallahs lived side by side, and that caste was not that big an issue as it was previously. But when I wanted to know whether inter-caste marriages were allowed in the village, he said no. He said that Thakurs would marry within their community and so would the Mallahs. He added that firstly, no one generally married outside one's community, and secondly if by chance someone did, it would lead to trouble. I realised that Chambal had not changed much. It was still enmeshed in caste problems. It might not be visible to outsiders but once you enter the place, you are bound to come across the undercurrents of caste based hatred. The Thakurs even now look down upon Mallahs (Majhis) and Gujjars. One wrong step and once again they would pick up their guns. Once more someone would jump into the serpentine ravines of the *beehed* and protest against injustices, turn into a ruthless *baghi*.

Unlike the garrulous Mahavir Singh, Puran Singh was more reserved. He carried his weight around. He told me that he owned two licensed rifles. I asked him since a number of their enemies were still alive, didn't they face any threats from them. I knew that blood for blood was the only rule in Chambal. Puran Singh replied that they did not face much threat because the charisma of the mighty Mansingh, the messiah of the poor, still worked magic in Chambal. *Dau* had no enemies. Puran's great-grandfather had never killed anyone without reason and had seen his enemies to their end. He had not left any descendent of his enemies alive. For all *baghis* in Chambal, *Dau* was an ideal. Also, many famous *baghis* had been initially trained by *dau*. So as Mansingh's descendants, they did not face many problem. On the contrary, they reaped the benefits of *dau*'s charisma. I further enquired Puran Singh regarding his political interests—whether he was a part of active politics, whom did they vote for, etc. He said that they supported the current king belonging to Bhadawars. Previously, this king was with the Samajwadi Party and all the Thakurs of the village voted for him. Presently he has joined BJP. Puran Singh was not too keen to speak any further. However, I came to know from him that the famous bandit of Mansingh's gang, Lokman Dixit alias Lukka was still alive. He was around hundred years old and was staying in a Jain area of a place called Waterbox in the Bhind district of Madhya Pradesh. His son's name was Ashu Dikshit. Puran Singh only knew this much about him. On enquiring about Rupnarayan or Rupa Maharaj, I came to know that he had passed away long back, but his family lived in the nearby village of Mahua. Puran Singh did not know who all were left in Rupa's family. I was a bit shocked. Mansingh had himself given the place of his deceased son Yashvant to Rupa, how could his descendants not keep an update on Rupa's family! I felt there was a catch somewhere. Puran Singh insisted that he only knew so much about Rupa or his family. I thanked him and got up to leave. Even this much information was good, I was sure to find the rest. As soon as we came out of the house, Mahavir whispered to me that one of the descendants of Rupa was the leader of a gang of robbers. Hence, they wanted to maintain a distance from that family and not share much information about them. However, during wedding ceremonies, the families got to meet occasionally. I realised that not just Puran Singh, no one in the village would divulge any information about the family. So, I decided to keep Rupa's family out of my work and yet kept a lookout for establishing any connection with that gang of dacoits.

We left the bike at Puran Singh's place. Our next destination was the house of Naresh Singh, son of Yashwant Singh, where the temple of Mansingh was situated. Every Sunday the villagers came there to worship and sang songs about Mansingh. The songs were composed by local minstrels. As we walked back there was a chill in the air. Suddenly Mahavir took out a plastic bottle and two pouches of water from his pocket. He made me sit on a mound by the roadside and offered a drink to keep the cold away. He said, 'I don't drink in front of my wife because she always gets angry and goes after my life. So, I have hidden a quarter and brought it here.' I refused it with a smile. He sat down on the roadside and gulped down half the bottle. Then he returned the bottle to his pocket. The more I saw Mahavir, the more confident I felt that I was not the only husband who is scared of his wife. Mahavir informed me that Naresh Singh's house was just a kilometre from there. We kept walking. The evening breeze in March was quite cold. It was fascinating to see that the eight feet wide road constructed under the Pradhanmantri Sadak Yojna was flanked on one side by a series of agricultural lands and on the other, the endless *beehed*. Occasionally, whistling sound of the blowing wind could be heard from the *beehed*—as if the *beehed*, like a siren, was beckoning me to itself. I kept on walking in a trance, my mind and body not in my control. Whenever I looked at the *beehed* and heard the whistle, my body felt numb—not out of fear, but thrill. I cannot explain why I felt so. Mahavir asked me to hurry. I asked him where that whistle was coming from. He laughed and explained that the earthen mounds of the *beehed* had many holes dug by snakes, rats, and earthworms. When the wind blows, air passes through these holes and creates this flute-like sound. Since the *beehed* is a vast and open expanse, a low valley in the Chambal basin, the whistle travels a long distance. Those who are new to the place are surprised by this sound but people belonging here are used to it. Mahavir suddenly left the road and started walking through the fields. We proceeded along the edges of the fields. From a distance, in a mango orchard, I could see a temple and a house similar to that of Mahavir's. In a few minutes, we reached that temple. Mahavir went to call Naresh while I sat on the temple pavilion to wait for them. The temple door was locked. Outside was an idol of Hanumanji smeared with oil and vermillion paste.

Naresh came and unlocked the temple gate. Inside was a huge marble throne on which sat the marble statues of Mansingh with his wife Rukmini Devi. On one side there was a laminated photograph of Tehsildar Singh, Mansingh's son and gang-member, and the latter's wife. On the other side was another laminated photograph, that of Sonvaran Singh, Mansingh's companion who was killed in the same encounter as Mansingh, and his wife. When I asked Naresh whether he had seen his grandfather, he nodded in affirmation. He said he had a very vague recollection of his grandfather because he was just a child when he was killed in police encounter. But he spoke about his *amma* or grandmother. He said that he and his brothers have been brought up by their *amma*, Mansingh's wife. After the death of their father and grandfather, Rukmini Devi emerged as the head of the family. Though an illiterate rural woman, she had a strong personality which helped her in facing even high-ranking police officials or important politicians with ease. She ensured that each of her grandsons received education as far as possible and got them into jobs. She also retrieved their confiscated land from the police. In later years, many of those police officials and ministers had accepted that even they were amazed by the personality of this woman. Such a strong personality perhaps could only suit the wife of Mansingh. She was the same woman who was so grief-stricken by the death of her eldest son that she sent her husband to avenge their loss. Though I knew most of these facts from my reading of *Abhisopto Chambal*, I asked Naresh a few questions.

When I asked him whether he knew anything about

the then home minister, Dr. Kailashnath Katju's visit to his grandmother regarding the surrendering of Mansingh, he burst with laughter. Then, looking beyond the mango trees within the temple premises, he added, 'Sa'ab, I have seen a lot since my childhood. Many important leaders and ministers used to visit *amma* with folded hands, asking her to make *baba* surrender. But she used to chase them all away. Once Kailash-ji visited us accompanied by Manohar Singh Mehta, the then home minister of Madhya Pradesh. He requested her to convince Mansingh to put down his arms and surrender. But she replied, 'Go and ask in the entire village whether my husband is a bad person. If even a single person says so, I shall ask my husband to put down his arms.' Thus, she chased them away.'

'How old were you then?'

'I must have been eight or nine, that's why I still remember it.'

This was the woman who could leave even the home minister speechless. But Naresh continued, 'Towards the end, *amma's* spirit was completely crushed in her fight to regain our land from the police. There used to be a time when no one in the village would charge her for anything. But then again, there was a time when she did not have even the fare to reach the police station. Those who used to bow down in front of her with respect or those who never looked into her eyes began misbehaving with her so much so that once she was thrown out of a jeep for not having the fare.' This is how perhaps the wheel of fortune turns—the wife of Raja Mansingh had to get off a vehicle for not having the fare!

Naresh Singh was the only son of Bharat Singh who was the son of Yashwant Singh, the eldest son of Mansingh. Naresh was in charge of the temple. He had two sons who looked after their farms. In between our conversation, Naresh's son, Govind Singh, entered with tea. Naresh informed us that after the division of property by the police, their family got ownership of the house, temple, and the adjoining land. By this time, it was almost 6.30 pm. Gradually many villagers started gathering at the temple courtyard. It was time for evening prayers in the temple that Tehsildar Singh had built with his own hands. After worshipping all the deities present in the temple, everyone sat in front of the statues of Mansingh and Rukmini Devi kept at the main door. In rustic Bundelkhandi dialect, they began singing songs of Mansingh's times. The songs were accompanied with *dhol*, *tasha,* and harmonium. While listening to the songs I kept wondering about one thing—this person, whom the entire country knew to be a ferocious robber, was still alive in the hearts of these people. Such was his charm and influence that even in the 21st century he was still worshipped in this small hamlet. And why shouldn't that be the case? He was everybody's *dau,* their saviour, the emperor, the Robin Hood of Chambal.

It was getting dark so I reminded Mahavir about returning. As Mahabir and I walked our way back through the fields, we could hear the song in the background—

He never looted the wayfarers
Oh friends, lend your ears
Did not leave his enemies alive
Blasting them off with bullets
Whichever village would Mansingh reach
There he was honoured
In such a way an era passed
Now hear what happened next.

We returned to Mahavir's house. His granddaughter came and served us tea and savouries. It was an open courtyard and even in the winter of early March, I was shivering. North India is generally not very cold at this time of the year. But as I said, on one side of this house was the *beehed* and on the other, the vast fields, the topography made it cold. Moreover, we were sitting under a wood apple tree. Mahavir noticed my state and asked his wife to give me a shawl. Wrapping the shawl around, I sipped hot tea. The *beehed* air was heady with the aroma of cooked mutton. I began discussing agriculture with Mahavir. He had never been to Kolkata so he asked me about the place. He enquired whether Kolkata had agricultural lands, what kinds of crops were grown there, etc. I informed him that Kolkata was an urban area but there were farmlands in various districts where farming was done well. Mahavir updated me that though potato harvesting wasn't good that year, they would get a rich harvest of mustard. As we kept talking, Mahavir's son arrived with a bottle of rum and a bowl full of hot and spicy mutton *kassa*. Mahavir kept sneaking sips at his country liquor. He hid the bottle under his shawl whenever his wife was around. Such spicy mutton and rum—it was altogether a novel experience for me. Rum was never my preferred drink—whisky or vodka was what I liked. But on this wintry full-moon night, under the wood apple tree in an open courtyard, in the company of mustard fields and a *beehed* drenched in moonlight, more than rum, I was tipsy on nature's beauty. I could never enjoy very hot food—each piece of mutton that went inside my mouth burnt my throat and left my ears fuming. But it was delicious. Mahavir's intermittent comments now irritated me. He kept saying, '*Arre*, why are you drinking like a woman, drink it up like a man. Just gulp it down in one go! What kind of small sips are you taking!' A wry smile was my only response to his words. It was with slight annoyance that I picked up my glass and went to stand near the road, facing the *beehed*. I wondered what could be better than spending this moonlit night atop the *beehed*, enjoying rum and fiery mutton. The full moon night of Holi was just ahead. A big round moon brightened the sky. I could not resist anymore and expressed my desire to Mahavir. He sharply retorted, 'Do you want to die?' Well, I could not understand why would anyone die by enjoying a drink atop *beehed*! But as the place was unknown, I kept quiet. Much later did I come to understand what Mahavir meant that day. Around 8:30 pm Mahavir's wife called us for dinner. In these villages, people have dinner by 8 or 8.30 in the evening and retire for the night. I, on the other hand, could never sleep before 2 or 3 am. We were still drinking when dinner arrived—a few small *puris,* mutton *kassa* and *tenti* pickle. Mahavir did not have the mutton. His dinner was *puri* and molasses. Being a gastric patient, mutton was off his diet. He ordered his elder son to get some fresh milk from the buffalo.

I finished dinner and walked around the courtyard with a cigarette on my lips. In the courtyard, there were two beds made on two charpoys. There was a quilt as well. There was a 60-watt CFL light glowing in the courtyard. But there was no power. Mahavir's wife informed that there was a power cut for most of the day, at least for 14 to 15 hours. They were completely dependent on batteries. After walking for a while when I came near my charpoy, I found Mahavir snoring. Since there was nothing else to do, I took out *Abhisapta Chambal* from my bag and began reading.

It was a unique experience. Six or seven decades back, Mansingh unleashed his reign of terror from one *beehed* to another. And in the present time, I was sitting in the courtyard of his house, reading his tales of adventure. Suddenly there was a sound and I saw a shadow approaching. 'Who's there?' Madhav, Somender's grandson replied, '*Bhaiya*, it's me. I had given you a ride this evening.' From where was he returning so late in the night! He said that he had gone to attend a wedding in the village. I asked him if he wasn't scared of robbers or wild animals. He assured me, 'There aren't any robbers in Chambal these days. Oh yes, there are snakes, but that is not a problem.' He then went towards his room. Howling wind, no houses within a radius of three kilometres, full moon night, the *beehed*, the farms and slight drowsiness induced by rum—eventually, I fell asleep. At around 3:20

am, a loud, jarring noise of a bike rudely woke me from sleep. In the darkness, it took me a while to understand where I was. Rubbing my eyes, I sat upright and after a few moments remembered that I was at a place which was 20 kilometres in the interior of Bah district, and that Bah was 80 kilometres from Agra—I was in the village of the legendary Mansingh, and that I had reached here this afternoon. Suddenly there was a bright headlight from the bike focussing on my face. I could not see the rider but I could make out that there were two of them. In a Hindi mixed with Bundelkhandi, a deep voice asked me, 'What happened *babu*? Did the noise from my bike wake you up?' By then there was another light in the courtyard—Somender Singh, the younger son of Mansingh's grandson had come out of his room. He asked the man on the bike, 'What's the matter Lallan?' Lallan responded, '*Arre*, we are going to Motiya's house, can we keep the bike here?' Somender nodded his head and they parked the bike on the opposite side of the courtyard. As they were leaving, they turned around to face me and said, 'You seem to be a new bird here!' Now I could see the stranger's face. He was six feet tall with whiskers stretching till ears. I was too stunned to reply. Somender replied, 'He is a journalist from Kolkata, and has come here to know about *baba*.' Throwing a spine-chilling glance towards me, the terrors of midnight walked away. Later I had come to know that he was Lallan Singh, grandson of Mansingh's closest companion, Roopnarayan Singh.

On the charpoy beside me, Mahavir, my host, continued to snore peacefully. I could not get any more sleep and took a stroll around the courtyard. Then I crossed the courtyard to reach the road, facing the *beehed* I relieved myself. It was around 3:30 am and the sky had started changing colours. I started to smoke knowing that there wouldn't be any more sleep for me. Suddenly I heard a voice, 'Are you scared?' I turned around to see Mahavir sitting on his bed with a *bidi*. I smiled. To scare me he pointed to something and said, 'Look at that.' I saw a snake around 10 to 12 feet long lazily slithering away, just a foot away from my bed. 'A python. Now these are the dacoits of Chambal. They are the ones who rule the *beehed* now.' To be honest, it made my hair stand on end. The snake had come from the direction where I had just gone a while back to relieve myself. Who knows whether that had woken it up from its slumber! Thankfully I was not walking around that place anymore. But was it even possible to get back to sleep after this? Mahavir had lied down again though. I spent the whole night sitting on the charpoy under that wood apple tree. However urgent be nature's call, I was not going to respond to it before morning. After every few moment, I kept checking my phone, waiting for sunrise. Only I know the way I spent the time between 3:30 and 6 am!

DEEPER INTO CHAMBAL

I left that morning just after tea. I was going to Bhind via Bah. From Jyot Kalyan, I had to cover a distance of 65 kilometres by bus. The night before, Mahavir had said he will give me a ride on his bike up to the place where we had met. But when I asked him in the morning, he tried to avoid me. By then, some old villagers had come to chat with him and were sitting on his charpoy. Mahavir suggested, '*Arre*, go to the main road, you will be able to get on a jeep from there.' I figured out that I would have to travel alone. When an elderly person asked me my destination, I replied that I would be going to Jyot Kalyan to travel to Bhind from there. Suddenly, Mahavir took me by surprise by suggesting an alternative and easier route. He asked me to take a jeep from here to Nadgaon, and then cross the river Chambal by ferry to reach Chattarpur. From Chattarpur another jeep would take me to Bhind. The entire journey would be 20 kilometres only. No need to take such a long route.

I reached the main road at 8:30 in the morning. But even after waiting for an hour and a half, I could not see any jeep. There was a police post at the turn of the main road where a few policemen were standing. I went near them. From their conversation, I gathered that they too would be travelling towards Jyot Kalyan. When I told them about myself, they said, 'Let's see when the jeep comes.' Suddenly there appeared a solution to our problem. From the field on the opposite side, a small toto-like van appeared. The policemen stopped it and got into it almost by force. I asked them to drop me till Nadgaon. Though they refused initially, when I said that I was a journalist from Kolkata, they agreed. They took me along with them. It was after a wait of two hours that I got transport. I perceived the acute problems of transportation in these regions. Compared to people of this region, we in the cities are far more privileged in terms of facilities. The policemen went on their way to Jyot Kalyan after dropping me at Nadgaon. They asked me to wait for another jeep there. There, too, I had to wait for an endless time. There was a small hut-like tea stall nearby where some old men from the village were drinking tea. I asked them about the frequency of jeeps and engaged in small talk. When they asked me about myself, I said I was visiting to write about Chambal. This caught their attention. A leader-like old man said, 'Are you a journalist? Then please write about us.' When I asked what I was supposed to write on, he replied, 'Write about our miseries.' I further enquired, 'Why, what miseries do you have? You have such wonderful roads, at every bend, there is a board proclaiming it to be part of Pradhan Mantri Sadak Yojna. That means that the government is working towards your development.' The old man laughed out loud and said, 'So even you got duped by the outer shine, isn't it?' I smelled a story there and immediately asked what he meant by that. He said, there are roads, but no transport, there are farms and there are crops, but farmers have no money. 'We have ration cards but the ration shop is so far that going there would cost us half a day's pay.' There were a few small, elementary schools, but for higher education one had to travel a long distance. The villages lacked good quality schools and colleges. After completing education in the village school, for colleges, students had to go to Bhind in Madhya Pradesh, crossing

River Chambal. Vast farming lands were being bought by big corporate houses to build farmhouses and expensive schools. But those schools and farmhouses were not for local people. Those were for the rich from the cities. After saying all these, the old man added, '*Sahib*, those who have land are still managing somehow, but people like us, who do not possess land but work on other people's fields, are living in hell.' I assured him that I would try to write their stories. I further enquired about the jeep. I had to go to Bhind by crossing the ferry and needed a jeep to take me to the ferry stand. The old man said that there was no particular time for the jeeps to arrive. Then he raised his hand to stop a bike rider who was just passing by and asked him to give me a ride to the ferry. He even refused to charge me for the tea. I sat behind the unknown rider and started my journey towards the ferry station of Chambal. Once again, there was *beehed* on both sides of the road, which at places were made of concrete, and at other places, it was kutcha. After travelling for about five kilometres, we reached the ferry.

Today's Chambal is the Charmanwati River of the past. The source of the river lies near the city of Mhow, near Indore, lying to the south of the Vindhya Ranges. From there it crossed Madhya Pradesh and Rajasthan before falling into River Yamuna at Etawah in Uttar Pradesh. Near Etawah is the confluence of five rivers—Yamuna, Chambal, and its tributary Kunwari, Kali Sindh, and Pahuj. In the local language, this place is known as the *panchnada*. The valley of Chambal and *baghis* of *beehed* have been sustained by these five rivers. The Chambal range consists of a large part of Uttar Pradesh, Madhya Pradesh, and Rajasthan. Places such as Mhow, Khera Rathor, Bah, Jalaon, Etawah, and Agra in Uttar Pradesh come under this range. Along with these, there are also the villages between Etawah and Kanpur—the Thakur dominated Chourasi Gaon (84 villages) and 113 villages of the Mallahs also fall in this region. Bhind, Morena, Gwalior, Datiya, Amba, Joura in Madhya Pradesh, Dhaulpur, and Bharatpur in Rajasthan—all these together were the habitats of the *baghis* of Chambal. Even the police and military were scared of tackling *baghis* by entering the *beehed* region. That fear exists even now. The forest-covered, serpentine lanes within the *beehed* were suitable for one person to pass at a time. It was not only difficult to look for dacoits along those lanes, but the chances of getting lost also posed a serious threat. Once lost, the person would keep roaming within the maze until rescued by somebody.

As far as one could see, there were extensive *beehed* and forests. River Chambal was flowing through the middle. The water was so clear that I could even see fishes below. The water would hardly come up till my nose but it had a very strong current. It was so swift that at times the boatman had to get down in the river to tow the boat in the opposite side. There was the ongoing construction of a bridge over the river for the past three years. But no one, not even the locals knew when it would be completed. On this bank of the river, a temporary shed, a cover over four bamboo poles, acted as a ticket counter. To cross to the other side was 15 rupees. Locals from Bah, Nadgaon, Mhow rode upon their bikes to the ferry station every day. They, along with their bikes, boarded the boat to cross the river and reach their places of work in Bhind, Madhya Pradesh, and returned the same way. In this way, the boat ferried not just humans but also cattle. Only those who owned camels could cross the river on a camel's back. On reaching the other side of the river with a lot of difficulties, I walked over sand to reach the jeep stand. It was merely a shadow of a stand with just two or three jeeps standing. As soon as I boarded one, it started moving. The road ran through the *beehed*. In the hope of some news, I struck up a conversation with my fellow passengers, the villagers. All men were dressed in *dhoti-kurta* and had a sandal or pump shoe covering their feet. I asked them about the situation in Chambal and whether *baghis* still existed. An elderly person among them, Yashvardhan Singh, exclaimed, 'Chambal is no more the same *babu.* Now it is a much better place. But there's no guarantee that it will remain so. The curse of the land here is such that it is not sure when will it pull someone to itself next.' Driver Ratan Singh added, '*Sahab*, Chambal has only one rule—blood for blood. Here if you leave your enemy alive, people will spit at you.' So saying, he broke into that same Bundelkhandi song that I had heard yesterday from the villagers of Khera Rathor—

> *Atharah baras lo chhatri jeebe*
> *baki to fir jeebe siyar*
> *jaake bairi jeebit baitha*
> *uwake jeeban rahe dhikkar*

They told me that dacoits were there, but not too many. A few gangs were operating still. And they at times surfaced in the dark of the night, particularly when they needed food. But they were nothing like earlier times. Police had almost wiped them off. As we travelled, I suddenly noticed a forsaken palace on top of a *beehed.* On asking I was informed that this was the Ater fort built by the Bhadwar kings. Its actual name was Devgiri Durg. Situated at a distance of five kilometres north of River Chambal, this fort was built by Maharaj Badan Singh. Once upon a time, they were patrons of dacoits like Mansingh and others. I remembered yesterday's conversation with Puran Singh when he had mentioned that they supported the current Bhadwar kings during elections. I asked my fellow travellers whether there were any stories about Ater fort. Yashvardhan said, '*Sahab*, this is a peculiar fort whose mystery remains unsolved. No one knows why blood drips from the '*khuni darwaza*' (murderous door).' I immediately smelled a story and probed further. Yashwant said, 'Even the kids here know this story.' I asked him to tell the story since there was still a long way to go. The story that I heard was beyond my belief.

THE MYSTERIOUS FORT

Ater Fort, situated in the banks of Chambal still carried the proof of the prowess of the Bhadwar kings. Blood dripped from the red door of the fort which was their symbol of valour. The spies who came to meet the king had to put a *tilak* of that blood on their forehead before entering the fort. There are hundreds of stories based upon that murderous, red door circulating today as well. Not only that, the place from which blood used to drip down is still marked on the door. This fort belonged to the medieval period and was famous as a symbol of valour and its beauty. It is situated upon a hill that has been referred to as Devgiri in the Mahabharat. That's why this fort is known as Devgiri Fort. It is a beautiful confluence of Hindu and Mughal architecture. Bhadwar King Badan Singh had started building this fort in 1664. It was in the name of the Bhadwar rulers that the Bhind area was also known as Badhwar region. Situated deep in the valley of Chambal, this fort was about 35 kilometres to the west of Bhind. This fort has an immense significance in the history of the Bhadwar kings. The chief attraction of this fort is the '*khuni darwaza*' (Murderous door), the palace of Badan Singh, *hatiyapor* (armoury), *Raja ka bangla* (the king's bungalow), *Rani ka bangla* (the Queen's bungalow), and Bara

Khamba Mahal (Palace of 12 Pillars). But the most discussed part of this fort is the *khuni darwaza*. According to a popular story in Chambal, as heard from Yashvant, the Bhadwar kings used to place the head of a slaughtered sheep at the top of the red stone door. There used to be a vessel just below the door in which the blood dripping from that head was collected. The spies could meet the king only after applying a tilak of that blood on their foreheads. It was only after that, that they gave the king significant information regarding his rule, kingdom, or enemies. Common people had no information regarding the blood that flowed under that door. Even today this door made of red stone is known as the *khuni darwaza* or the bloody door. Recent historians have found that the Ater fort had been mentioned even in the Mahabharat, though from a historical perspective this fort is only 350 years old. There are many apocryphal and legendary stories associated with this fort such as the stories of hidden treasures as well as black magic. The greed of local people is largely responsible for such a ruinous state of the fort. They have dug up the fort in various places, hundreds of people have broken its walls and floors in search of the treasure trove. Hence the fort is in ruins now. Presently the fort is abandoned, desolate, lonely. There is no sign of maintenance, except a signboard from the archaeology department. At night it becomes the den of crooks who engage in gambling here. In this huge fort, there is just one caretaker. The past glory of the Bhadwar kings is now in shambles due to complete neglect.

During our conversation, the jeep stopped. The crowded bazaar-like area was the final stop of the jeep. Before starting with work, I needed to find shelter. Bhind in Madhya Pradesh was more significant than Uttar Pradesh and Rajasthan because this has been the birthplace of a larger number of dacoits. Asking my way around, I managed to leave the crowded area and reach the wide road. Just ahead of me was a hospital and an inter-state bus terminal. But I could not find a hotel. Finally, taking help from a policeman I checked into a lodge that fit into my budget. The first room allotted to me was so small that only a bed and a mirror were somehow fitted into it. There was an attached bathroom, too cramped up for space. They asked me to adjust for a day. By the next day, there would be more rooms available and they promised to give me a better room.

Somehow, I managed to freshen up. The lodge also had a sweet shop. I had tea with *samosa* and vegetable curry, and retreated into my room to sleep for a couple of hours. The twin terrors of python and the bike rider snatched my last night's sleep. Food was secondary, but the task for which I was here required an adequate amount of sleep. My experience at Khera Rathod had made me aware that in Chambal, I shall have to rely more on my feet than any other form of conveyance. To maintain that kind of energy, sleep was essential. I had reached Bhind at 11 am. So, I could sleep till afternoon. After that, I needed to plan the rest. There were three people whom I wanted to meet here—Mohar Singh, Malkhan Singh, and Lokman Dikshit or Lukka Dacoit. The last one was one of the closest associates of Mansingh, who was by his side even during Mansingh's encounter.

As soon as I reached Bhind, I called up Ekram da and informed him of my whereabouts. After waking up I called him up once more to discuss my plan with him. I told him that I planned to spend the day moving around to get some information about the three people on my list. I wanted to move forward only after procuring their addresses. I also told him that since Lukka Dacoit lived quite close to the hotel where I was staying and was too old to venture out of his house, I would be visiting him last. He suggested I draw a proper plan and move accordingly. I also needed to know how far Morena and other places were from Bhind. Among all the places on my list, Morena was the most interesting one because that place had temples completely hidden from public view. There were several crocodile sanctuaries there in the water bodies adjacent to those temples. And then, of course, there was Baghi Madho Singh, one of the most popular *baghis* of Chambal. But I was not much concerned with the dacoit Madho Singh, there were other reasons for my interest in him. After his surrender and subsequent imprisonment, Madho Singh was released from jail without any opportunities for rehabilitation. He had to spend his time in abject poverty. He was a close friend of Tehsildar Singh. They were responsible for a huge number of *baghis* laying down their weapons in front of Jayprakash Narayan in 1972. There was another fact about Madho Singh that made me curious—in his last years he had earned his livelihood by performing magic tricks along the streets of Benaras. He had once even contacted the great magician Senior P. C. Sarkar in Kolkata to learn magic. He had also acted in a few mainstream Hindi movies as an associate of the main villain. Interestingly, when Jayprakash Narayan had refused to agree to Madho Singh's proposal regarding surrendering of *baghis*, Madho Singh even secretly come to Kolkata to meet Jyoti Basu. But Jyoti Basu too refused him help. I was fascinated by all these various aspects of his character. I learnt more about Madho Singh from the timekeeper at Bhind bus stand, whom I had befriended during my stay, than from all the information from *Abhishapta Chambal* and *Behed, Baghi, Banduk*.

As soon as I woke up, I got ready, took my *jhola*, and came down to the sweet shop. I met the caretaker of the lodge and informed him about my purpose in Bhind. His words were quite disappointing. After a series of expletives, he lamented, 'Where are any dacoits these days! The ones you see now are all wicked. Previously they used to rob people at gunpoint and now some of them have become leaders and are looting people even without guns.' He only informed me that Mohar Singh lived in a place called Mehegaon at a short distance from there. But he refused to divulge anything more.

So I walked towards the bus stand to find out buses plying to Mehegaon. I was also looking for information regarding Malkhan Singh. At the bus stand, eating *chole bhature* from a wheeled cart, I met a person and began talking to him. I enquired about Mehegaon and was told that it was around an hour and a half's journey from Bhind. That septuagenarian observed me and said, 'You don't seem to belong to this place. Why do you want to go to Mehegaon?' I told him my intention and came to know that he was the timekeeper of this bus stand and would let me know the timings of buses that ply to Mehegaon. But the bus to Mehegaon was in the evening so he ordered two cups of tea from a nearby tea stall and said, 'All you journalists run after Mohar Singh but never tell people the story of Madho Singh!' I became curious and asked him to tell me more. The timekeeper, Jagrup Singh, then started telling me, 'Madho Singh was an all-rounder among the *baghis*. I was quite close to him. If you have time then come along with me.' He brought me to his small room, the timekeeper's room, and began telling the story of Madho Singh. In each turn of the story, there was a surprise hidden.

MAGICIAN DACOIT MADHO SINGH

Life in Chambal was quite opposite of the tranquil waters of that river. Just as all waters of the *beehed* find its final home in the river Chambal, all *baghis* too ended up near Chambal, no matter where their points of origin were. But it was for the first time, Chambal found a *baghi* whose trigger-friendly fingers as well as his intelligent mind worked equally fast. Even after 40 years, he was still a legend amongst people. In his life, he had been a male nurse in the army, a dacoit, a magician, and an actor. In each of these roles, he had left his mark. Contrary to the popular saying in Chambal that dacoits did not follow their minds but their hearts, he was an exception who did not act under impulse but followed his mind. Madho Singh's story started as one of revenge and ended in his becoming a *baghi*. But he was no ordinary *baghi*. He was one whom Chambal either referred to as 'Chambal Sarkar' or as 'Masterji'.

The one who used to tend to the wounded and injured, turned into a ferocious, blood-thirsty *baghi* of Chambal when his own heart was brutally hurt. In the history of Chambal, Chambal Sarkar Madho Singh's name began being taken in the same breath as that of Mansingh, Rupa, Lakhan, or Mohar Singh. He began by killing his enemies. But thereafter he unleashed such a reign of terror that police forces of three different states was up on their toes to end him. In 11 years, there were hundreds of cases filed against Madho Singh and his gang. But when that very Madho Singh, who always managed to flee from police attacks, surrendered himself to the police, 500 other dacoits came with him. Even after that Madho Singh appeared before the public in a new avatar—not as 'Chambal Sarkar', the dacoit, but as a magician. He became so famous that wherever he performed, a crowd gathered around him. I was mesmerised listening to the tale of such a magician.

The village of Garia Baghraina came under the Pinahat Police station in the Agra district in the region of Chambal that belonged to Uttar Pradesh. This village beside the *beehed* was no different from other villages in the area. Once you enter the village, you find only a few dried wells and a temple under a very old tree. In front of that temple was a door to a house. Looking at that door no one would imagine this was a place that birthed a dangerous dacoit. Madho Singh was born in a farmer's family. Their plot of land was not too big but they were well respected in the village. He had spent a happy childhood in the village. I was quite surprised to know from Jagrup Singh that he had spent his childhood with Madho Singh. Looking at my bewildered face, Jagrup Singh explained that Madho Singh was a few years senior to him but they belonged to the same village. They had been playmates in their childhood. Jagrup further said that he too had joined Madho Singh in *beehed* but he could not stay there for long and returned to normal life in the village. I realised I was talking to an old companion of Madho Singh who has been mentioned in *Behed, Baghi, Banduk*. The old man said that right from his childhood, Madho had just one mantra that he had to do something big in life. But he did not choose a wrong path to achieve easy success. Instead, he chose the path of hard work. The old man ordered more tea and I offered him a cigarette. After lighting his cigarette, the old man resumed his tale. Madho's performance in studies and sports got him recruited in the army. He joined Rajputana Rifles Medical Core as a male nurse. Until this point, everything was fine. Madho Singh had just started laying the bricks for a pucca house in place of the kutcha house in his village. But some of the people in his village could not tolerate his improved situation. It was almost seven years that Madho Singh was serving as a male nurse and people were getting increasingly jealous of his progress. Around this period, Madho Singh took a long leave to come to his village. After returning home, with the help of medical knowledge that he acquired during his training in the army, he started treating patients in the nearby villages. Good behaviour and excellent communication skills made him a success here as well. This success also increased the number of his enemies in the village. One day these very people brought a charge of theft against Madho Singh. Though he tried to defend himself, there was no one in the village to listen to him. In this region of Chambal, people believed that both law and police followed the one with silver shoes, that is they always favoured the rich. Madho Singh could not fathom which way his fate was pulling him. No one was willing to believe his words. Immediately after the allegation, there was a conspiracy to murder him as well. Madho Singh understood that his hopes for a normal life in the village had come to an end. After tolerating all these for some time, the day Madho Singh lost all his patience, he got hold of a rifle and went to the gate of his enemy's house.

Gunshots intimated villagers that once again someone had let loose their anger to seek revenge. Madho Singh's name was already there in police files because of his jealous fellow villagers, but now Madho Singh got himself included in the most-wanted list. Enmity within the village, his hot-headedness, and the waters of Chambal ultimately dragged Madho Singh into the *beehed*. The gangs of Chambal always await the entry of a new lawbreaker. Madho Singh had taken the law into his own hands and he needed the shelter of Chambal. In those days there were a few dozen gangs present in Chambal. Madho Singh went and joined the gang of Janga or Jangjit Singh's gang. That gang was one of the most feared gangs in Chambal during those days. Madho Singh worked for this gang for a few days. But he was also trying to find his footing there. Though Madho Singh was part of the medical core of the army, he had received arms training as well. Military discipline too helped him. And very soon he gathered a few followers to form a group of his own. Gradually this gang became one of the biggest gangs due to his intelligence. A few face-off with police towards the end of 1950s had finished off several big gangs. Mansingh, Rupa Maharaj, Putli Bai, Sultana dacoit, and several such brutal *baghis* were dead. In such a situation Madho Singh decided to become not just the leader of a gang but the ruler of entire Chambal, thus he became Chambal Sardar. His gang started procuring new kinds of weapons. Meanwhile Madho Singh, once again, attacked his village and finished off all his enemies. He killed eight people in his village in one visit. And by that act, he closed whatever slim chances he had had of his return to his village. Madho Singh and his gang got involved in one crime after another. He started from Uttar Pradesh and gradually extended his base into the Chambal regions of Madhya Pradesh and Rajasthan. They were chiefly involved in loot, robbery, and murder. Madho Singh knew that whenever he would operate from his base, police would keep an eye on him. Moreover, by 1960s, government started providing villagers with licensed firearms to face the dacoits. Many times villagers even stood up against dacoits. Hence, they had to often incur losses. So, after much thinking, Madho Singh came up with a new idea, the idea of *pakad* or kidnapping. He kept kidnapping people one after the other and it became one of his favourite means. This made Madho Singh infamous throughout Chambal.

Around this period there was another powerful gang operating in Chambal—that of another dauntless *baghi*, Mohor Singh. Very soon Madho Singh's fame became parallel to that of Mohor Singh. He became the first *baghi* who turned the act of kidnapping into an art. It was the easiest way to earn. He laid his traps in such a way that his victims themselves walked into them. Thus, Madho Singh secured his reign in Chambal.

The more I heard about Madho Singh, the more surprised I was. My curiosity kept increasing and I kept on prodding Jagrup for more. Jagrup smiled in response and said, 'Have patience *sahib*. This is a never-ending tale. Whatever I say of Madho will fall short of his actual life. What a man he was! What all he did in his life! His life had as many colours as that of a movie. Wait, let us drink some more tea.' This time I stopped the old man and said I wanted to pay for the tea. I got up and went to the nearby tea stall to get tea and cigarettes. Madho Singh's story was resumed once again.

It was Madho Singh's reign in the jungle during those days. The police could only increase the price of his head, nothing more. In those times, thousand rupees meant a huge lot. Prize money for Madho Singh's head touched a few lakhs. He became the dacoit with a price of one and a half lakh rupees—dead or alive. Madho Singh set his headquarters in the jungles of the Shivpuri region. He started devising innovative ways to extort money after a kidnapping. Not murders or robberies, Madho Singh became desperate in his methods of kidnapping. Instead of one or two people, he started kidnapping in groups and that got the police extremely worried. He even kidnapped groups of people from picnics. An example will better explain the innovative ways of Madho. Once, he dressed as a senior officer of the police and went to a group of people picnicking near a *kund* in Rajasthan. He went to one of them alleging him of being involved in some incident, and pointed at another person accompanying him as his informer who identified that person. Simultaneously, he had also informed the local police station. The policemen who came to that place, rounded up all the men present there and presented them in front of Madho Singh. But, on seeing real police, the one playing the role of the informer panicked and ran away. Immediately Madho Singh decided that he would kidnap all the people present there. But how would he kidnap so many people in front of the police! So Madho Singh decided to take help of the police itself in this kidnapping. He told the policemen that all these people had to be transported to the headquarters for interrogation and for that they must arrange for a police truck. When the police hesitated, he used his military mannerisms, learned during his stint at the army, to convince them. Once the truck arrived, the men were forced to board the truck. After some time Madho Singh and his cronies felt that a truckload of sheep that was following them was actually the police in hiding. Immediately, Madho opened the window behind the driver's seat and shot the driver of the vehicle following them. The bullet went through the driver's chest, killing him, and the truck met with an accident. Immediately news spread through the city that Madho Singh, disguised as police, had kidnapped a number of people. The police were in an uproar. But by then, Madho Singh had vanished with his hostages. Now it was just a matter of time before the call for ransom, which of course arrived soon.

After narrating up to this point, Jagrup paused. He caught his breath and smiled at me, 'Do you know the identity of the informer who had run away?' I shook my head, the old man laughed aloud and said, 'That was me. I had then newly joined Madho Singh's gang. Everyone is scared initially. And who won't be scared to see actual police! Of course, Madho Singh was an exception. I, too, got scared and ran away. But there was nothing called fear in Madho Singh. He fooled the police and escaped with the picnickers. But later Madho Singh had scolded me. He told me, "If you are scared, then *beehed* is not the place for you. Go and surrender yourself to the police. But even then, you will not survive because I shall kill you."'

Contextually, it was Jagrup-ji who had provided me with the address of Ajay Mittal of Shivpuri, Madhya Pradesh, whom I had gone to meet later. That person was an octogenarian, one of the kidnapped picnickers. Ajay-ji still vividly remembers how Madho Singh kept him in the jungle for two months. The dacoits used to walk through Chambal throughout the night. After walking barefoot through thorny bushes of the *beehed* for almost a month, the hostages were in a bad state. Only after reaching the Murena forest did they get to wear shoes. Ajay-ji remembers wherever Madho Singh went, other gangs from that area came to pay him respect. According to their status, the *baghis* would take off their shoes at a distance, before meeting him. Many of them often asked this ex-army person to display his shooting skills. Madho Singh used to tie a cloth over his eyes and shoot at a *bajukay* (a thin iron pipe-like thing) kept between three men. Ajay-ji claimed to have witnessed this several times but he had never seen Madho Singh's target waver. He remained with Madho Singh till his ransom money of 10,000 rupees reached the *baghis*. According to him, villagers of different villages of Chambal supported Madho Singh. Wherever he went, the villagers shared with him their tales of woe and he would try his best to help them.

To come back to Jagrup's tale, after a while I told Jagrup that I must have been disturbing his work, so I should leave. He replied, 'What's there to do! Keep sitting here throughout the day and note down the timings of the buses. Stay here, the story has just begun.' Lighting another *bidi*, he resumed. Tales of Madho Singh's kidnapping became famous even beyond Chambal. He had kidnapped more than 500 people. In the police records, he and his gang were mentioned as 'E2', or Enemy no. 2. Police were desperate to catch him. They spread their informers all across the jungles and therefore Madho Singh thought of changing his *modus operandi*. But before he could act upon his plans, he had a major confrontation with the police. That day, even the sky turned grey due to heavy firing. In that encounter, which lasted for about 72 hours, only Madho and one of his companions could escape. All others died in police firing. After this, there was news that Madho Singh's body has been riddled with bullets. But a person from his group went to inform his family that the Master survived the attack and managed to escape. Most of the gang members had learnt shooting from him, so he was popularly addressed as Master by them. That encounter completely eroded Madho's confidence and he changed his operating style again. He took shelter in Vijaypur forest where only a handful of people could reach him. Even the members of his gang could not reach him directly. The nature of Madho Singh's work also changed. Around that period, just a letter from Madho Singh used to send shivers down the spine of many affluent people. There was no dearth of new weapons for Madho Singh. By 1970 Madho Singh was using weapons that the police could procure only after 1971. But by now, Madho Singh was tired after 11 long years at Chambal. Though he was living in the forest and running his gang according to its rules, in his heart he wanted to move out of the *beehed*. In those days, he often used to spread rumours about his own death and secretly went to the city to spend some time with his family. Or he would bring his family to stay with him for some time. Face-off with the police had become a daily affair. The combined forces of Uttar Pradesh, Madhya Pradesh, and Rajasthan police were frantically trying to end the dacoits in Chambal. At successive operations, dacoits were being killed. The police had also been successful in breaking through the networks of informers that the dacoits used. Many police informers had infiltrated the gangs as well.

Jagrup-ji came to an abrupt halt. A conductor had come to

get his bus timing recorded. After dealing with him, Jagrup-ji wanted to call someone. A few minutes after the phone call an old man arrived. He was quite stout and though he seemed to be of Jagrupji's age, he did not look that old. The most attractive part of his appearance was his moustache, long and thick. He introduced the stranger as a retired police officer of Madhya Pradesh, Mr. R.L. Verma. Then Jagrup-ji told him—'He is a journalist from Bengal. I was talking to him about Madho Singh. But without you, the story will remain unfinished. Hence I called you.' Then he turned towards me and said, 'Meet the officer who had planned that operation against Madho Singh's gang that lasted for 72 hours and had broken Madho's backbone. Listen to the story directly from him.' Some more tea was ordered for all of us.

The police had planted informers in Madho's gang too. Along with it, they engaged him in one confrontation after the other. One such operation had been planned by Mr. Verma himself which went on to become one of the biggest encounters in Chambal. In the encounter that took place on 13th March 1971, police had killed 13 of the most important associates of Madho Singh which included names like Kalla, Garh Singh, Chintaman, Babu, and Vishambhar Singh. Police took special care to ensure that this news reached Madho Singh, and hence they aired it on the radio. After listening to this news, Madho Singh commented that whatever was left of the gang had been finished by this encounter. After that incident, Madho Singh realized that there was no guarantee of his life in Chambal. So, he finally decided on ending his *baghi* life forever. But that was not an easy task. There was a saying in Chambal that in a *baghi*'s life there are just two dates—the date in which he jumps into the *beheed*, and the date when his body is brought to the city wrapped in neem leaves. The *baghis* who were killed in encounters were brought to the city wrapped in neem leaves. Madho Singh realized that to save himself from the neem leaves he needed a good plan. Within a few days, he came up with one such plan. The story that I next heard from the old man was more fascinating than any fairy tale or Bollywood movie.

Madho Singh decided to surrender. The greatest of the *baghis* in Chambal was contemplating taking the shelter of the law. On the other hand, the police wanted to finish off Madho Singh. In such a situation, cunning Madho Singh came up with a plan that no one could do anything about. He did not plan to surrender alone. But he wanted to do it with 500 more dacoits from Chambal. He immediately started working towards the fulfilment of his plan. He first wrote a letter to the then home minister, Gulzarilal Nanda, and a few other bureaucrats. But he did not receive any reply from them.

Madho Singh remembered that once Acharya Vinoba Bhave had made some dacoits surrender. *Baghis* like Lokman Dixit and many others had laid down arms in front of him and returned to normal life. In 1971, a forest contractor called Ram Singh reached the *ashram* of Vinoba Bhave and told him that the notorious dacoits of Chambal were once again willing to surrender and return to normal life. But Vinoba Bhave expressed inability to help and told Ram Singh that he was an old man with failing health and he could not undertake a journey to Chambal. He advised Ram Singh to meet Jayprakash Narayan and offered to write a letter to him. Ram Singh agreed and took the letter. But in those days leaders like Jayprakash Narayan were not easily accessible. When Ram Singh reached Delhi, Jayprakash Narayan was in Kashmir, so Ram Singh left for Kashmir too. But even there he could not meet him. Then he came to know that Sucheta Kripalini knew the address of Jayprakash Narayan. After a lot of effort, Ram Singh met her and procured the address. Finally, one day the forest officer Ram Singh reached Jayprakash Narayan's house in Patna. On meeting him, JP asked, 'Who are you? And what is your relationship with the dacoits in

Chambal?' Ram Singh said that he was a forest contractor but when he saw that JP remained non-committal, replying in just a yes or a no, he stood up and in a very deep voice said, '*Sahib*, my actual name is not Ram Singh, but Madho Singh.' JP was completely stunned. He could only ask—'Are you the same Madho Singh on whose head there is a prize of two lakh rupees?' Madho Singh replied, 'Yes, I am that same person.' But Jayprakash Narayan refused to help him and asked him to leave. That day Madho Singh left JP's home but did not lose hope.

Suddenly Jagrup-ji said, 'Babuji, aren't you from Bengal? There you have a fine leader called Jyoti Basu.' I was surprised. What did it mean! We were talking about Madho Singh. How did Jyoti Basu's name crop up here? Seeing my reaction, both Verma-ji and Jagrup-ji laughed aloud. He said, 'Let me tell you, that day I had accompanied Madho Singh to JP's house. But when things did not work out, we returned to our hotel. That very night we decided to go to Bengal.' It was still not clear, so I said, 'You can of course go to Bengal. But what has that got to do with Jyoti Basu?' I was confounded. What was the relationship between this dacoit of Chambal and the man who governed Bengal for 23 years?

Seeing my bewilderment, Verma Sahib came to my rescue and told Jagrupji, 'Nath Sahib is unable to make out anything. Why don't you narrate the whole story?' The story that followed was too fantastic to be true. I have never written about it before because there is no proof of the story. Who would believe the amazing tale that I had heard from those two strangers, sitting in a dingy room, in Bhind district? But now that I have undertaken to write my entire experience of Chambal, I won't leave anything out.

Jagrup-ji said that the very next morning, almost at dawn, they left for Kolkata. On reaching Howrah they stayed at a very small hotel. They stayed there for almost two and a half months. Meanwhile, they started establishing contact with the Naxalites of Kolkata. Madho Singh had hoped they he would be eagerly accepted by the Naxals because he had a lot of modern weapons. Then he could easily mingle with the Naxalites. But he failed there too. The Naxalites did not accept him in their group. Then he somehow managed to procure Jyoti Basu's address. Then one day at around 11:45 pm they reached Jyoti Basu's residence, 55B, Hindustan Park. They could finally meet him. But Jyoti Basu said that without any direction from his party he was unable to do anything. Moreover, there was a lot of difference and distance between Bengal and Chambal. So, he said he was unable to do anything for the dacoit sardar. 'Do you know, we had bought some *rasgullas* and sweet curd from a shop over there and taken those for him? But he did not accept those gifts from us.' The tale was leaving me more and more bewildered. How could the disparate elements like the dacoits from Chambal, the Naxalite movement of Kolkata, and the legendary leader Jyoti Basu come together in a single tale! Anyway, after being refused help from all quarters, Madho Singh returned to Chambal again. He got in touch with Mansingh's son, Tehsildar, and sought his help. Then the two of them once again went to meet Jayprakash Narayan. Before that visit, the duo had convinced the other dacoits of Chambal to surrender. Who was not there in that group! The terror of Chambal, Mohar Singh, too, was a part of it! Madho fell at Jayprakash's feet and said there were about 500 dacoits who wanted to lay down their arms in front of him. But they did not want to rot in jail, neither did they want to be handcuffed. They should not get life sentences. This time JP was more open to discussion and agreed to go to Chambal. But there were doubts in Madho Singh's mind—what if their demands were not met? Then Jayprakash assured him that in case the government refuses to accept their demands, he would sit on a fast till death for them. That made Madho trust him completely. He returned to Chambal. Preparations for surrendering began at

Pagara dam, in Jorai village in Madhya Pradesh. 14th April 1972 was finalised as the date for surrender. Inadvertently it slipped out of my mouth that 14th April was my birthday too. I could not explain what was going on within me. I was born on 14th April 1983 and was listening to stories of an event that had taken place exactly 11 years before my birth! It almost seemed that I was predestined to reach Chambal and write the story of the *baghis*. Otherwise, why should I, an IT engineer from Delhi, become a journalist! I was not supposed to join this profession as I was leading a comfortable life in Delhi. Since I reached Chambal, there has been a series of coincidences. The day I reached Uttar Pradesh was the day Mansingh was released from jail and walked towards Kheda Rathod; the day I reached Khera Rathod and stood at his door after so many years was the date on which he had held his son's hand and jumped into the *beehed* through that very door. I would be a witness to Mahavir Singh's refusal to drink water at his kin's place because the latter did not respect women and was a gambler. And then, 11 years before, on the same date as of my birth, a historic event had taken place, that is, the largest number of dacoits laid down their weapons. I felt that Chambal and I were tied by an umbilical cord, how else could one explain my meeting these people in such a strange land? All seemed to be a part of the greater design. I met Mahavir as soon as I got down at Jyot Kalyan, then Jagrup-ji and Verma Saheb in Bhind. But I neither had any address of any of the *baghis* nor the names of their villages. But everything seemed to be a part of the plan. Well, enough of digressing, now back to Jagrupji's narrative.

Just as Madho had kept a few conditions for JP, JP too kept a condition for Madho. He was aware that a large number of dacoits had surrendered before Vinoba Bhave. So, he placed the condition that not just the dacoits from their gang but also other gangs should surrender on that day. Madho agreed to this seemingly impossible condition. But the biggest deterrent to this task was the most feared dacoit Mohar Singh. In the history of Chambal, the highest award had been declared on Mohar Singh's head and he was the one who ran the biggest gang of dacoits. Not only that, but the largest number of police encounters were also against Mohar Singh's gang. Mohar Singh was the most dreaded name of Chambal at that time. He knew that after so many murder cases in his name, either the noose or a bullet from the police was awaiting him. Madho Singh embarked upon the mission to convince Mohar Singh. Several meetings and proposals later, Mohar Singh started trusting Madho Singh and finally even agreed to his proposal. In the last meeting, Madho Singh had put his hand on his son's head and swore that JP had promised to fast unto death if the police or the government failed to keep their demands. After that Mohar Singh did not hesitate any more. Murena's Pagra dam went into a festive mood. National and international media buzzed around the place. No one at Chambal had seen such a gala affair in their lives—500 dacoits surrendering at one go! There were thousands of people who had come to see the dacoits. And then there were political leaders, ministers, police personnels, and national and international journalists. The dacoits arrived in jeeps. Some of them posed with their guns for the journalists. There were no restrictions. Amid such a carnival, Madho Singh and Mohar Singh along with 500 other dacoits surrendered their arms at the feet of Jayprakash Narayan. But how is it possible that Madho Singh would surrender and there will not be anything new in it? So just before the surrender, after the government had accepted all their conditions, Madho Singh also sought compensation for the families who had been the victims of these dacoits. As a result, the hatred that people bore towards him was changed to love and gratitude. An open-air jail was constructed in the Moongawali village of Madhya Pradesh for these dacoits. Madho Singh served his term there. Jagrup-ji paused and pondered, 'Had it been some other *baghi*, his story would have ended here itself. But Madho always had some new idea stirring in his mind. And he embarked on another new project.'

The next part of Jagrupji's story was equally enthralling. In 1961, Madho Singh had visited the Senior P.C. Sarkar at his residence in Kolkata. That was the period when he had lost interest in Chambal. He wanted to learn magic from the maestro but the master refused. Yet that did not deter Madho Singh. He learnt magic from another magician in Kolkata. Jagrup-ji could not recall his name any more. The once infamous Chambal Sarkar who invoked terror among people was now entertaining them with his magic. After retiring from his life as *baghi* he also acted in a few movies. Some of those movies were never released and those which were released did not do well at the box office. Towards the end of his life, Madho Singh used to perform magic shows in various streets of Varanasi. In the early phase of his career as a magician, Madho Singh became quite popular and was invited to perform at various places of Uttar Pradesh, Madhya Pradesh, and Rajasthan. His magic skill mesmerised people. Madho Singh's life is an incredible but true story—an ordinary person turning into a *baghi*, and then that *baghi* converting hundreds of other *baghis* into normal human beings. Verma Sahib said that most of the police officers believed that Madho Singh had a crucial role in that historic surrendering of the *baghis*. Such an impossible thing would not have happened without his active participation. This was the journey of the army male nurse Madho to Baghi Madho to the great magician Madho. He had spent years in financial distress, supporting himself through his earnings from magic shows. He used to allow the police free entry to his shows. In 1991 Madho Singh died. Jagrup-ji said, 'Do you know *saheb*, Madho was a film buff. He worked in films too. Once, during his *baghi* days, he had called a producer from Mumbai and gave him 5,000 rupees to make a film on him. But that producer ran away with his money. Then Madho kidnapped one of the relatives of that producer and extorted four times that amount from him.' Jagrup-ji laughed!

It was just getting dark outside. But the more I heard, the more amazed I became. Jagrup-ji asked me to come back to the bus stand the next morning around 10 am when he would get me on the bus to Mehgaon. From there, the next day I would proceed to Bilao, the old village of Malkhan Singh. From there he had started his life as a *baghi*. Jagrup-ji said that he would extend me every possible help throughout my stay in Bhind. I thanked him and stepped onto the roads of Bhind, leaving the two old men in that small room. Once upon a time best of the *baghis* had walked along these roads of Bhind. This was the Bhind that evoked terror in the rest of the country.

After returning to the hotel, I freshened up. I was so engrossed in Madho Singh's story that I felt the need to unwind my thoughts a bit. I needed to come out of it to plan my next steps. I was hungry. But this time I did not want to go to that sweet shop, instead, I wanted to explore the nearby eating places. After wandering along the road for some time I located a fast-food joint and immediately entered it. It was a small shop. There was a boy taking orders whom I asked to get me a sandwich. It would take some time for the sandwich to arrive, so I sat there and kept browsing the pages of a Hindi magazine. Suddenly a very tall and well-built man arrived there. At a glance, anyone could easily mistake him to be a hero in one of the south Indian movies. He was around 6 feet tall and was wearing a pair of jeans trousers with a shirt tucked into it. He had a huge moustache. As soon as he entered the shop, he started giving orders to the boy. I chanced a look at his waist and my eyes almost popped out of their sockets. There was a revolver hanging from his waist. At first, I thought he must be a police officer. I kept staring at him. He went away after a while. I immediately called the boy and asked him about that strange person. He said it was the owner of the shop, Ravi Singh. 'He moves around with a revolver?' I probed. 'Yes, *bhaiya* always carries a gun.' I wanted to know why. 'Just like that!' That person came back to the shop and on seeing the boy talking to me gave him a scolding. I intervened, '*Bhaiya* please don't mind. I was the one talking to him.' The man turned towards me and asked, 'Who are you?' I told him about myself and then asked, 'Why do you carry a gun?' Ravi Singh looked at me for a while and said, '*Bhai*, you don't stay here so you won't understand. Without guns, moustache, and tractor, a person has no status here. We move about with arms to show our status. I have a licence for firearms. I also have some unlicensed guns.' I continued, 'Don't the police say anything?' Looking at my surprised face that handsome Rajput replied, 'The police only gave it to me. We are the Choudharies. Such things are usual here. This place is not as calm as your Bengal. Here, people are hot-blooded.'

Just imagine, moustache and guns becoming imperative to maintaining status! The sandwich arrived and I continued my conversation with Ravi-ji while eating. I asked whether dacoits were still a problem in Chambal. Ravi-ji informed me that dacoits are not as much a problem as they used to be. A bigger problem is the *beehed* because it is gradually eating up agricultural land. The police have more or less solved the problems of the dacoits. Chambal is now more peaceful when compared to before. But that doesn't mean that there are no dacoits any more. I asked him if it was possible to meet any of those dacoits or get in touch with them. Ravi-ji gave a mysterious smile and in a peculiar voice said, 'You want to meet dacoits? Then you will.' He did not wait even for a moment, and rode away on a bullet that was parked outside the shop. I tried making sense of his words if they contained any hidden meaning.

I had to return to my room soon after as there was nowhere I could have gone so late. Also, I could not have just roamed around in that unknown place. There was no television set in the room. So, my phone was my only solace. I had come to such a place where not even a tea stall remained open after 7 pm. Just then one of the boys of that lodge came and told me that a bigger room was available. Since I had asked for one such, I could take a look. I went along with him. The room was quite big. It was just beside the street and had a sliding glass window. That same boy brought my luggage from the previous room. But he did not leave. I thought he was expecting some tip so I put a 10 rupee note in his hand. He smiled, but still did not leave the room. I asked him if there was anything he wished to say. The boy hesitated a bit, looked around cautiously, and said, 'You went to Ravi-ji's shop to ask about dacoits?' I was quite surprised and asked him how he got to know about that! He replied, 'Ravi-ji is not a nice person. Don't talk to him about such things.' I was quite irritated. Do I have to take permission from this boy from a hotel about where to go and whom to talk to! I retorted, 'How does it concern you? Why don't you mind your own business?' The boy said, 'Shut the door properly before sleeping.' I told him that I needed tea at night, so he could get me a cup of tea from their sweet shop downstairs. He said that after seven there won't be any tea available but if I wanted, he could get me a flask full of tea which I could have at my convenience. I gave him a 50 rupee note. He brought tea in a flask and a cup. I sat beside the window, sipping tea, and kept wondering—this was the road where once Malkhan Singh, Mohar Singh, and others had roamed around. At a short distance from the hotel was Lokman Dikshit's residence. I kept pondering over the history of Chambal and its many dacoits whose names were enough to evoke terror across the country. Just a little farther was the cursed river of Chambal. This river which flowed through three states, covered a distance of around 900 kilometres and finally merged with the Yamuna. But the story of Chambal was longer than the length of this river. Chambal originates from the Mohu district of Madhya Pradesh. Until the river enters Dhaulpur in Rajasthan, those living along its banks do not see rebellion in its course. After Dhaulpur, the river's character changes. On one side of this river is Rajasthan and on the other is Madhya Pradesh, and then on one side Madhya Pradesh and Uttar Pradesh on the other. And spread along these hundreds of kilometres are stories of the dacoits and *baghis*. And I have come to Chambal and its *beehed* to find the hidden truth of this land—the true stories behind names like Mansingh, Dongar, Batri, Rupa Maharaj, Lukka Daku, Lakhan Singh, Amritlal, Mohor Singh, Malkhan Singh and many more. It was an unending list and difficult to find its beginning or end. Chambal valley was not just replete with the smell of human cruelty amidst explosives and guns, but it also had an extraordinary tradition of female dacoits. Though the *baghis* did not want to include any women in their gangs, there are love stories in Chambal which have given birth to dacoits like the first woman dacoit of Chambal, Putli Bai. The tradition that began with Putli Bai was carried forward by the older ones such as Phoolan Devi, Kusuma Nain, Seema Parihar, and to the present-day dacoits like Renu Yadav, Sarala Jatav, or Neelam Gupta. A trip to Chambal has so many colours that it often becomes difficult to separate fact from fiction.

While thinking of these things I did not realise when I had fallen asleep. Quite late in the night, there was a knock at my door. I thought it must be the boy who had come to call me for dinner because the main door was closed after 10 pm. After that, it won't be possible to leave the hotel. But as I rubbed my eyes and checked the mobile, I saw it was 2 am. I was quite surprised—no one would come to call me for dinner this late! Then who was banging on the door? I had forgotten to switch off the light before sleeping but in a hotel, no one would ask me to switch it off. I was drowsy and felt quite irritated. I got up from my bed to open the door, thinking that I would give the boy a piece of my mind. But I did not know that this knock would stay with me forever. Nor did I know that the next 25 minutes were to be the most outstanding moments of my life, whose horror was not to leave me any time soon, so much so that even after returning from Chambal I slept fitfully for quite some nights.

Grudgingly I left my bed and opened the door and was suddenly pushed by two hands. By the time I regained balance, there were around ten people in my room. Before I could say anything, a strong voice shook me up completely, 'Oh *patrakar babu*, you were too keen to meet the dacoits, so we have come. But don't worry we have come to meet you and talk to you. After all, you are our guest. Hope you are not having any troubles here?' By now I had steadied myself and looked around to find ten dacoits including a woman in front of me. Ravi-ji, the one whom I had met in the fast-food shop was also there. Suddenly his parting words came back to me and I could understand the meaning behind his mysterious smile and words. The hotel boy was also there. He had been forced out of his sleep. Ravi-ji sat on my bed and said, 'Come, sit, there is nothing to be so scared about. We have just come to meet you.'

Wasn't there anything to be scared about? At 2 am there were around ten dacoits in my room. And he said that there was nothing to be worried about! Ravi-ji pointed towards a man who was six feet tall with a clean shaved face and had pistols on both sides of his waist and said, 'Meet him *patrakar sahib*, he is Babuli Kol, right now the greatest terror of Chambal. And she is Gauri Jatav. She had first joined Nirbhay's gang but currently, she is the second in command in Babuli's gang. These two are now ruling Chambal.' By then the dacoits were sitting on my bed and the stools in the room. One was sitting upon the table. It was as if they were chatting in a local club and I was their guest. Ravi-ji ordered the boy to bring some nice tea for everyone and that I was their guest so

I should not face any problem in the hotel. Once the boy left, Ravi-ji extended a 50 rupee note towards me and said, 'It was a mistake on my boy's part. You are our guest. How can we charge money from you?' I objected, 'I should pay for what I have consumed.' But Ravi-ji forced the money into my hand and said, 'Chambal is infamous throughout the world but it knows how to take care of its guests. However bad a name we might earn for ourselves outside, for us our guests are of utmost importance.' I did not argue any further. Who knows, it might just irritate them enough to put a bullet through me. Hence, I took back the money. Babuli did not look like a dacoit at all. On the contrary, he resembled a Bollywood hero of my younger days, Vivek Musran. Like a boy of my age with back brushed hair and a stout physique. Except for his eyes, nothing else could make him look like a dacoit. I had not seen eyes colder than his. When he saw me looking at him, he extended his hand. We shook hands. His hand was so strong that my arm started aching. What comparison could be there between a dyspeptic, undernourished, 5'5" journalist from Bengal and this six-foot-tall and armed dacoit from Chambal! What was the fault of this poor hand of mine! After shaking my hands Babuli laughed out aloud, '*Arrey*, your hands are as soft as that of a woman, *babu*!' Everyone laughed aloud at his words. By then tea had arrived. Babuli picked up one of the glasses and said, 'Tell me *saheb*, why did you want to meet us?' I told them about my intention. Hearing that Gauri lashed out, 'All you media people, do you think that we jump into the *beehed* because we wish to?' There could be no reply to this. I tried to explain myself a bit more to Babuli and Gauri. I told them that I had come to understand the people of Chambal, to understand why they turn into dacoits, and to see their life in the *beehed*. As I was speaking, I saw Gauri taking a cigarette from my packet. She said, 'I hope you don't mind me taking a cigarette, *saheb*?' She did not even wait for my reply to pick up the lighter lying near it and lit the cigarette. No words could describe my state at that point. I said to myself, even if I objected, who was going to listen to it. In a moment you can kill me with one of your bullets. Finding me speechless Gauri continued, 'Girls in your city must be smoking, right? I have heard that quite a few women journalists both smoke and drink.' I tried to manage the matter by pasting a smile on my face. She was about 5'8" tall, dark, had a red tilak on her forehead and her lips were red due to continuous chewing of betel leaves. Wearing tight jeans and t-shirt with a shirt over it but with buttons open and knotted at the waist, she looked like a dacoit diva. Around 27 years old, Gauri was not extremely beautiful but she was attractive enough to draw people's attention towards her. The way she walked and talked or conducted herself, she could easily fool city girls. To change the topic I asked, what is your area of work? This time Ravi-ji answered. 'Do you have any idea what prodigious dacoits they are! Babuli's head carries prize money of 5 lakh and Gauri's 2 lakh. Both of them belong to the Chitrakut region.' Following is an account of these two dacoits by Ravi-ji.

Babuli was the Badshah of the Chitrakut region. He was the fifth dacoit from this region who had a price of five lakh on his head. Before him, Dadua, Thokia, Ragiya, and Balkhariya had a price of five lakh rupees on their head and all of them had lost their lives to police bullets. Now Babuli wanted to be a dacoit greater than his predecessors. Shooting someone simply to maintain the atmosphere of terror was child's play for Babuli Kol. Now that his head is priced at five lakhs, his name spells terror for the residents of Chitrakut and Patha region. Babuli considers the one-time terrifying dacoits like Dadua, Thokia, Ragiya, and Balkhariya as his masters. At present there are around 47 cases filed against him for murders, attempts to murder, kidnapping, etc. Babuli came to the limelight when he shot five persons of a family in one go and wreaked havoc in Dodomafi village. After that incident, terror and Babuli became synonymous. Prior to that, he was in the gang of Balkhariya. The dread of Chambal, Balkhariya, had more than 25 cases of murder, loot, and kidnapping to his name. The police forces from Uttar Pradesh and Madhya Pradesh were desperate to catch him. Finally, on 2 July 2015, he was killed in police encounter. During the encounter, Balkhariya had told his associates, 'If I die, the police should not get my body.' He had also said that after his death Babuli should be the leader of their gang. After the death of Balkhariya, Babuli declared that they were going to avenge the death of their leader. He also brought the corpse of their leader to a secret place and completed the cremation. He did not let the police get their leader's body.

In recent times, in April 2018, Babuli had a run-in with the police in the forest of Atarsui, under Markundi Police Station. But he managed to escape from there. After getting a secret tip, the police surrounded the forest from three sides under SP Manoj Kumar Jha's leadership. They confronted Babuli near the Atasurai forest. Though the police chased them, Babuli and his gang took advantage of the forest and fled from there. The police confiscated large number of utensils and food from that place. According to the last bit of information, Babuli had ran away into the forests of Madhya Pradesh.

Gauri on the other hand was from Uttar Pradesh. While she was studying in college, she had been kidnapped by Nirbhay Singh Gurjar. Like Neelam Gupta or Sarala Jatav, Gauri too became Nirbhay's keep. But after staying in his gang for about a year and a half, Gauri managed to escape from there. But by then all doors of her returning to society were shut. During her stay in the *beehed* she had got acquainted with Babuli. Compared to the womaniser Nirbhay, she preferred Babuli. So finally, she joined Babuli's gang. Now she was second-in-command in this gang.

While conversing, I asked Babuli if I could take a picture

of Gauri and him along with the gang. He remained quiet for a while. Then, taking out the pistol from his waist he pointed it first towards me and then towards the window. After continuing like this for five whole minutes he said in a chilling voice—'*Patrakar saheb*, we came here to meet you because you had expressed such a desire to Ravi-ji and because you have come from such a distant place. We are not film stars but dacoits. Even the police do not have our latest pictures. We are talking to you because you have come to know about Chambal from so far. And also, because Ravi-ji has accepted you as his guest. Ravi is a very good friend but you must not write about me.' By then I was scared for my life. What a mistake to ask for a photo, and now there are chances I myself would turn into a photo. Looking at my condition Gauri laughed out loud and said, 'Why are you scaring him you sister fucker! Leave it! Come let's take him on a trip to *beehed*. Patrakar *sahib* too will get to see *beehed* and find out what the fuck we do there.' By then I was sweating profusely. It will be the end of my story if they take me to the *beehed* and kill me there. I protested, 'No, no, it's quite late to go anywhere! I have learnt about you all, that in itself is a huge experience for me. There is no need for anything else.' Gauri sidled close to me and whispered, 'Don't be scared. We have accepted you as our guest. We shall not kill you. Come along, we shall have some fun and frolic and drink with you. You will also remember what grand king and queen of Chambal you had met. Come now.' And she immediately stood up. I was about to put my phone and purse in my pocket when Gauri shook her head. So, I just picked up the lighter and my packet of cigarettes and came out of the room shutting the door behind me. Babuli then told the boy, 'Listen, we are taking him with us now and shall send him back tomorrow morning. But no one should come to know of it.'

When I came downstairs, I saw the jeep parked in front of the hotel. Ravi-ji was driving and Gauri and Babuli sat in front. I along with the other members of the gang took our seats in the back. Past midnight the jeep tore through the main road of Bhind. Everything else was completely silent. Bhind was deep in slumber. No one even came to know that a Bengali journalist was travelling with a group of dacoits towards the *beehed*. There was the slight chill of March. Moreover, in spite of all their assurances of not killing me, I was sceptic and scared. So, I felt colder than usual. I have had various kinds of experiences since yesterday—I had spent a night in the house of one of the greatest dacoits of Chambal, heard the story of a dead and erstwhile dacoit from another ex-dacoit, and now I was heading towards the unknown in the dead of the night, surrounded by dacoits who had a heavy price over their heads. Though I was extremely scared, I tried to cheer myself up by remaining positive. Let's see what happens at the end—I kept saying to myself. If I have to die, then so be it. But if I survive, this would be an experience of a lifetime.

Terror-stricken, I did not even keep track of time in the jeep. When it stopped, I saw that we had reached that river bank from where I had boarded a jeep for Bhind in the morning. Once again, we crossed that sandy stretch to reach the river ghat. The gang of dacoits started walking along the banks of the river, taking me along with them. After walking for about ten minutes, we reached a *beehed*. We climbed up to reach the space between two *beehed*s and started walking. The dacoits were using four huge torches to light up the way. The moonlight and the yellow light from the torches mingled together to add to the mystery of the night. There were short thorny bushes along the way as well as along the walls of *Beehed*. I, unused to this place, got a few scratches as I walked with them. There were even holes at places. I kept tripping as I walked. I had often run away from home and have consequently faced many dangers too. But this was the second time in my life that I found myself in a truly life-threatening situation.

In 2005 I had gone to the tea estates of Darjeeling and Gangtok to work there. While in Gangtok I faced an earthquake where I was trapped in a tea store on the ground floor of a house. That tea store was also the place where I was staying. Due to the earthquake, all doors and windows were blocked and I did not know how to come out of the room. The owner of that house had to break open the window to rescue me. I had a broken arm and leg.

But even at that time, I was not too scared of death as I was during this walk. Once my foot got caught in one of the holes and I tripped and fell. 'Oh, you city boy, this is not the *pukka* road of your Kalkatta.' I had to bear such jibes from Gauri. My hands and legs were itching badly. We had been walking in the *beehed* for about 15 minutes, but to me it seemed almost fifteen hours! Fear and tiredness had left me completely parched. I did not know how long I had to walk. This was how they crossed miles across Uttar Pradesh, Madhya Pradesh, and Rajasthan! How could they walk so much! After walking a bit more we reached a clearing. There were about four tents on one side of that space, some wooden boxes were arranged in a circle, and the *beehed* all around. In the middle, there was a heap of branches and twigs for lighting a fire. I did not know where this place was but since we had not crossed the river, I was sure that we were still within Madhya Pradesh. Suddenly Babuli said, 'Welcome, *huzoor*, to the home of the poor! Please take a seat and take a look around my palace. Sky overhead, *beehed* below, and all around there are wild animals and snakes—this is how I sleep!' Had this been a dialogue in a Hindi movie, it would have earned loud claps and whistles. Soon some of the dacoits retired to their tents. Ravi-ji and some others sat on the ground or upon the boxes. I too sat on one of them. They lit a fire. With the help of a dynamo, a bulb was also glowing in one corner of a tent. Moreover, that being a full moon night, there was no dearth of light. It was windy too. The presence of the river nearby made the air humid. I felt cold. I looked around properly. This was the place where the dacoits had set up their home. There were utensils here and there and there was a drum full of water too. They had arranged bricks to make a kiln as well. Babuli called out loudly to Gauri, '*Arre* you woman, we have a guest with us, why don't you show him some hospitality! Serve him some food and tea.' Gauri emerged out of one of the tents and replied, 'Don't give him tea so late at night. I have something else for him. *Patrakar babu* has come to our place for the first time. Let us show him the kind of hospitality that will make him happy and he will praise us even after returning to Kalkatta.' She went back inside the tent but came out almost immediately. All of us were sitting in a circle around the fire. Gauri came out with a bottle of rum and a few aluminium foil packets. Then she ordered someone to get glasses. I had not noticed till then but now that I saw, my eyes popped out of their sockets—in one of the tents, there were rows of guns! Most of them were the latest models—AK47, double barrel rifles, guns with telescopes, and so on. The more I saw, the more scared I felt. Gauri sat very close to me on one of the wooden boxes. My sixth sense told me that sensing my fear, Gauri wanted to tease me even more. She knew that the closer she would try to come to me, the more scared I would be and she would then further poke fun at me. She was trying to flirt with me and I was increasingly losing my nerve. I was unaware of how her actions were being interpreted by Babuli. But the more I moved away from her, the closer she sat. Finally, in irritation, she blurted out, 'Why are you getting so scared you sister fucker! I am not a witch from the forest who will eat you up!' Then she asked me, 'Will you take me to Kolkata to show me the city?' I smiled somewhere between a yes and a no.

Rum had been poured into the glasses. Gauri understood that I was not going to give in to her taunts, and calmed down a bit. Babuli said, 'Please make yourself comfortable Bangali *babu*. It is Gauri's habit to keep pulling legs but she is not bad at heart.' By then, another dacoit had switched on a tape recorder. Each one was holding a glass. It was just yesterday night at Mahavir's house, I was so drawn towards the *beehed* that I wanted to climb to its top with my glass of drink. I wanted to drink under the moonlit night. And just one day later, I was sitting in the moonlight flooded *beehed*. On one hand, the temperature was low, on the other, there was heat from fire and rum. I kept sipping my drink slowly. Everybody picked up pieces of meat from the foil pack and continued eating. On realising that I was not eating anything, Gauri picked up a piece and offered it to me. Then she picked up her glass and kept humming a tune. Though this moonlit *beehed* and rum was what I was dying to enjoy last night, I could not soak myself in it now that the opportunity had arrived. Ravi-ji and Babuli sat on a side and were discussing something earnestly. But without paying attention to them I asked Gauri, 'You all are staying in *beehed*, but aren't you scared of the pythons here?' Her response was quite odd, '*Saheb*, the wild animals are not as ferocious as the human beings outside the forest.' I asked her the meaning behind this. 'Leave it *Saheb*, what's the use!' I could smell a story behind her words and asked her, 'Why did you come to the *beehed*?' After keeping quiet for a while, she said that she had not come of her own volition. She was a student of B.A. first year in the Goswami Tulsidas College at Chitrakut. She was born in a lower caste farmer family. I interrupted, 'You are a Yadav, how can you belong to the lower class?' This made her laugh, 'Not Yadav, Babu, Jatav. It sounds like Yadav. We are farmers belonging to the lower caste.' I further interjected, 'But if you are poor, then why did Nirbhay kidnap you? He must have known that he won't get much money!' Gauri informed that kidnappings were not always for money. It was also a way of taking revenge on one's enemy. The son of the village *pancha-*

yat used to disturb her continuously and wanted to sleep with her. She kept refusing him. One day she had also slapped him in college for misbehaving with her. The village elders had held a court that day to decide on the issue and since it was the fault of the *panchayat pradhan*'s son, the verdict went against him. But the *pradhan* could not forget that insult. He paid Nirbhay to kidnap Gauri. One day when she was returning from college, Nirbhay kidnapped her. He raped her for days. During that time there were two more women in his gang—Neelam Gupta and Sarala Jatav. Nirbhay had kidnapped a young boy, Shyam Jatav whom he introduced as his son.

Nirbhay had married the famous dacoit beauty, Kusuma Nain. After that, he married another dacoit diva, Seema Parihar. Then in 1994, he married another woman called Basanti. But Basanti got a chance to escape. Nirbhay kept on searching for her and finally in 1999 he found her and killed her and her brother. Thereafter he kidnapped Sarala, the 11-year-old daughter of Basanti's brother. After two years he married her to Shyam but kept on raping her. It was from this point that Sarala became popular as a dacoit-beauty in Chambal. Nirbhay had kidnapped another girl from the Auriya village of Itawa district in Uttar Pradesh. Her name was Neelam Gupta. He then married her as well. Then in 2003, he kidnapped Gauri. Nirbhay loved to seduce women. He did not leave even the wife of his adopted son. In between all these, Neelam and Shyam got together and secretly conspired against Nirbhay. They also fell in love with each other. Neelam and Sarala were the biggest attractions of Chambal by then. Sarala was fair, beautiful, and intelligent, while Neelam, though dusky, was no less attractive. But Sarala had become second in hierarchy within the gang. Nirbhay depended more on her. Therefore, whenever Nirbhay was away, she led the gang. Neither Shyam nor Neelam could accept her authority. Neelam maintained a secret relationship with her stepson and kept provoking him. Among the wedded wives of Nirbhay, along with Kusuma Nain, Seema Parihar, and Basanti, there was Munni Pandey, Parvati alias Chamko. There was no count of the number of wives Nirbhay had. There was a period when around two hundred villages of Chambal lived in his terror. He had committed more than two hundred murders and kidnappings. There was a prize money of two and a half lakh rupees on his head. Then in 2005, one day Neelam with the help of Shyam ran away. They left the *beehed* and went to the police to tip them about Nirbhay. Nirbhay died in that police encounter. Shyam and Neelam surrendered themselves to the police. Neelam was sentenced to an imprisonment of twelve years. Sarala too surrendered herself.

Gauri had run away from Nirbhay before his death in 2005. But all roads to her home were blocked. When she went back to her village from the *beehed*, she was tortured by the police for days. Though she had learnt to shoot, she had never been involved in any robbery or murder. Her work was mainly cooking and taking care of the dacoits. Yet, she lost her reputation due to her days in the *beehed*. I asked her, 'Why didn't the police believe you?' She explained, 'Why would they believe me? The dacoits of Chambal involved the entire gang in their activities. Wherever they went to commit robbery, they left behind a chit of paper containing the names of all the members of the gang.'

So, without even doing anything, Gauri got involved. After returning to her village, she had to face harassment not only from the police but also from the village headman. At every step, she had been insulted as a prostitute and as one of the women of Nirbhay. Repeatedly the *panchayat* met to decide her case and again and again she was insulted. Then one day, unable to bear any more, she got in touch with Babuli and ran away to the *beehed*. She improved her shooting skills, committed murders and robberies. I asked her whether she was nervous during her first attempt. She laughed, and then said, 'No, there was a little bit of hesitation but by then the world had filled me with so much hatred that I could have rained bullets on anyone. What was my fault? I wanted to study. My results were good too. I wanted to get a job after my studies so that I could make my parents' life comfortable. But this bastard of a fate dragged me here.' This was normal in Chambal, whatever human beings planned, their fate decided otherwise.

Standing on top of the *beehed*, I could see a blurry river Chambal flowing slowly. Nothing mattered to it. There was no turbulence in it. The lives of these human beings did not have any effect on it. Its only job was to keep flowing across ages and be a silent witness to the tragic stories of these people. It had witnessed the tragic fate of Gauri too—the story of a *salwar kameez* clad, shy, 18-year-old girl who once had dreams in her eyes. The Gauri who was once the apple of her parent's eyes, now wields the gun and shoots strings of abuses. The girl who once shivered to see blood, now plays with blood. This was probably the fate of Chambal and its people. No one knew who would next be sucked into the *beehed*. Even today Chambal was carrying the burden of curse of a woman from Mahabharata. Who knew how many more Putli, Phoolan, Seema, Kusuma, and Gauri would be sacrificed! I was lost in my thoughts when suddenly Gauri patted on my back and said, 'Come on *yaar*, what's the point in crying over my fate! I shall follow it wherever it takes me and then one day everything will be over. But why spoil today's fun buddy! I quite like you. Babuli is busy now, so I am going to have a great time with you.' Oh, Mother Goddess, spare me! Who does not want to fall in love! But then falling in love with such a firebrand woman! Long live my Bengali wife. Though at times I do call her Phoolan Devi, due to her short temper, she suits me a thousand times better than this bandit queen. At least during a quarrel, she won't press the trigger. Both of us returned near the fire. The tape recorder was playing 'Baby doll *main sone di,*' a popular Bollywood number. Babuli got up and started dancing with Gauri. After they stopped dancing, Babuli said, '*Patrakar bhai*, Ravi will drop you at the hotel. Please go back with him. Let me romance a bit with my darling, who knows when the police bullets will shred us. But just one thing—whatever you heard or saw here, never write about it. If you do so…' He left it at that and went inside with his arms around Gauri. Was I crazy! It was enough that I was returning from the lion's den alive. Who would want to get exposed to further danger! Other dacoits, completely drunk, lay asleep on the ground outside the tents. Ravi-ji and I returned by the same path. Once again, we walked along the river and reached the jeep. The jeep sped fast, leaving Chambal river, Babuli's den, and the *beehed* far behind. When Ravi-ji dropped me at my hotel, it was 5:45 am. Before driving away, he once again cautioned me that I must not write about my rendezvous with Babuli and Gauri in any newspaper because they were extremely dangerous. Bhind highway was slowly stirring to life at that time. In various shops, they were lighting *chulhas*. Some were busy making tea, fritters, and *jalebis*. *Jalebis* were also being fried in the shop that belonged to this hotel. I could also see tea boiling. On seeing me return, that hotel boy ran up to me, surprised, and asked, '*Babuji*, hope everything is alright?' I patted his back saying that all was well. I told him that he must not wake me at seven now but at 9 am though I knew sleep would elude me. I was feeling exhausted. I went straight to the bathroom and turned on the shower. There were cuts in quite a few places where blood had clotted. I had also hurt my ankle by tripping. Warm water washed the tiredness of my body. But the tales of misery and woe that I had heard last night—would it ever be possible to wash that away?

After bathing, I lied down on the bed. My body was dead tired. Sleep overpowered me but I could not shut out the scenes from the *beehed* from my consciousness. I kept on pondering over those and then at some point, fell asleep. Around half-past nine I was woken up by a knock on the door. I recalled hearing this knock a while back as well, but in my sleep, I thought I was watching scenes from last night and hence did not get up. When the knocks became louder, I finally woke up. I opened the door to find the hotel boy whom I had asked to call me. He said he had come to call me twice before too but there was no response. He asked again, 'Hope you are okay *saheb*?' I smiled and assured him. The boy's attitude towards me had changed overnight. Till last night his deference was the kind that was generally shown towards all boarders. But today I could discern a change in his attitude towards me. He was probably thinking that I was some important personality whom dacoits pick up and return to the hotel with care. I asked him to get some tea and went to freshen up. I kept wondering whether I should let Ekram da know about last night's incident. I wanted to tell him but was scared as well. I kept sitting with the phone in my hand, unable to decide—Babuli, Raviji, both had warned me against writing about them. Tea arrived and along with it, two *samosas*. The boy's name was Ram Singh. He placed the *samosas* on the bed and said, '*Saheb*, you did not have anything since last night, so I brought these.' There was a terrible ache in my limbs. The bruises were also demanded attention, else they might cause trouble later. I gave Ram some money and asked him to get me a bottle of Dettol and a strip of Calpol tablets. As I sipped tea I planned the day's schedule. After leaving this place, I needed to reach the bus stand and meet Jagrupji. From there I would take a bus to Mehergaon where I would look for Mohar Singh. After that, if time permitted, I would go to Bilao, Malkhan Singh's village. I tied my right heel with a crepe bandage that was there with me. Last night I had twisted my ankle while walking with them in the *beehed*. Though it was not swollen much, there was severe pain. Meanwhile, Ram returned with medicines. He was very happy when I asked him to keep the change. I applied Dettol on the cuts and took medicine and went to the reception to return the keys. No one asked me anything. Perhaps, no one except Ram knew about the things that had happened in their hotel the previous night.

I took a rickshaw to the bus stand and met Jagrupji. He told me that I had half an hour before the bus left. I gathered more details regarding Bilao village from him. Bilao was the birthplace of the famous dacoit, Malkhan Singh, the place from where he had started his life as a *baghi*. I asked Jagrup-ji about the route to Bilao though Malkhan Singh did not live there anymore. Jagrup-ji did not know his current address. Therefore, today's plan was Mohar Singh and after that, if time permitted, Bandit Lukka. Jagrup-ji got me into a white bus and asked the conductor to help me get off at Panitanki near Mehergaon. I was sitting near the door, on the window seat. These buses were not like those of Delhi or Calcutta. They did not halt every ten or fifteen minutes, but wherever they found passengers. The first stop came after about half an hour of riding. The bus waited there for at least seven minutes. People got down for tea and to smoke. I also got down for a cup of tea. The conductor came and stood beside me so I offered him tea as well. He enquired whether I was a relative of Jagrupji. I told him about myself. On hearing that I was working on dacoits, he said that he was a resident of Bilao, the village where Malkhan Singh was born and from where started his life as a *baghi.* He gave me various information about Malkhan. He said that to catch Malkhan, a police station was also set up in the village though it does not exist anymore. The rubble of a police barrack was the only symbol of its existence. He gave me some more details about the dacoit which helped me later. After a while, he dropped me at the Mehergaon bus stand. But after getting down I could not understand which way to take. I asked at a shop. The shopkeeper pointed at a water tank at a distance and asked me to enquire there. After reaching there I asked another shopkeeper who asked me to wait for some time.

Then suddenly from a group of children returning from school he called one and asked me to accompany him as he would take me to Malkhan Singh's house. That kid who took me to the *baghi*'s house was probably in standard three or four. We went through narrow, serpentine lanes. I kept talking to the child. He asked me, 'Are you Bholu's guest?' I was quite surprised—now who was Bholu? The child emphasised—'My friend. I am taking you to his house!' I told him that I wanted to meet Mohar Singh for some work. The child told me that Mohar Singh was Bholu's grandfather. After walking for a while, we reached a house with a bluish wall. He pointed at it and said that it was Bholu's house and he ran away. What now! All doors of that house were closed. I did not know anyone. I took a closer look at the house. On both sides of the house, there were two long porches. At the centre, there were a couple of steps leading to a door. I kept knocking at that door. After some time, a woman, with a foot-long veil covering her face, opened it. Unable to see her face, I did not know how to talk to her. She was also holding a baby. Anyway, I told her that I had travelled a long distance to meet Mohar Singh. The woman told me that he had gone to the market. When I asked him when he will return, she told me that he spends time gossiping with his friends in the bazaar so it would be evening before he returned. It was just 12:30 then. How to pass such a long time! I called up Ekram da who suggested that I waited till Mohar Singh returned. But by then the woman had closed the door. The entire neighbourhood was soaked in silence, all the houses had their doors shut. It was afternoon and I was sitting on the porch outside. It felt extremely uncomfortable. What would I reply if someone suddenly came up to ask me what I was doing there! I decided to explore around the house. I walked along the porch. There was a huge iron gate. Beyond that was a wall. I walked back and started walking around the house from this side. I found another door and a flight of stairs beside it. I ran my eyes around the place and saw that the houses here were similar to those in Old Delhi, all huddled close to each other. There was a three-inch-thick brick wall as the boundary. Most of the houses had plasters coming off them. They were concrete houses, but they looked quite ugly, like an unplanned cage of bricks and mortar. There was no one on the road. But how long could I keep waiting! So, I knocked once again. This time a small boy opened the door. From a distance, I could see a very old man with a walking stick approaching me. Around 6'3" tall, he had a thick moustache and high-powered glasses. Though he used a walking stick, his backbone was straight. As he approached, I found him closely resemble the photos that I had seen on the internet. This was Mohar Singh, the one whom I was so keen to meet, the notorious dacoit who had once been the terror of Chambal. But when did he return! I did not see him enter the house. He asked, 'What do you want? For the past one hour, I have been noticing you walking around my house. What is the intention?' Though he was around 80 years, his deep baritone could put even Amitabh Bachchan to shame. Just by listening to his voice, I felt nervous. Somehow, I managed to utter, 'I am a journalist from Bengal. I wish to interview you.' He waved his hand in the air, making light of my words, then walked down the porch up to the iron gate, and pushed it open, 'Come with me.' On entering the gate, I saw a paved courtyard and on one side of it, a cattle shed made of bamboo and tarpaulin. There were a couple of cows there. In the centre of the courtyard was a cot. By then a young man of about 24 years and two boys had come and stood near us. Chambal's legendary dacoit Mohar Singh sat down on the cot and beckoned me to sit beside him.

MOHAR SINGH

In the fifties, there was a sudden uprising of *baghis* in Chambal. *Baghis* like Mansingh, Rupa, Lakkhan Singh, Gabbar Singh, Sultana stomped around Chambal creating an atmosphere of extreme fear. By the beginning of the sixties, many of these *baghis* had either been killed or their gangs had been reduced to a smaller size. But in the sixties, Chambal found a new name that surpassed all others in its terror. That name was Mohar Singh. The villages of Chambal have given rise to enmities which in turn have created thousands of *baghis* who found shelter in the *beehed* of Chambal. But sometimes such stories of rivalries have also created *baghis* who went on to become Badshahs of Chambal. This is the story of that *Badshah* who had the largest dacoit-army in the history of Chambal. After Mansingh, the biggest name in the Chambal region was that of Mohar Singh who had more than 150 dacoits under him. In the police files of Uttar Pradesh, Madhya Pradesh, and Rajasthan, he had been designated as Enemy No.1 or 'E1.' In the sixties, Mohar Singh's gun became the rule of Chambal and his words were the law. By looking at the police records in the police stations of Madhya Pradesh and Uttar Pradesh, I have come to know that in 1960 Mohar Singh had committed his first major crime and he had created such an environment of fear that the police were scared to even set foot in Chambal. The dacoits in the gang of Mohar Singh could easily escape from police attacks. He had such a strong network that the moment the police stepped into the forest, he came to know about it. According to information received, Mohar Singh would quickly adjust strategies as required. The journey that started in 1958, the first time when Mohar Singh's name was entered in police records, and it ended with his surrendering along with several other dacoits. But by then Mohar Singh had officially become a dacoit with a prize of two lakh rupees on his head and his gang was worth 12 lakh. The value of this amount in 1970 would surpass a crore in terms of rupees today. Apart from the 25 murder charges, there were about 315 cases against Mohar Singh. His was the longest journey in the history of Chambal which ended with his sudden decision to lay down his arms. Mohar Singh was an ordinary young man living in a small village in the Dang forest area of Chambal. They owned some farmland. Though there are numerous stories of enmity and revenge scattered throughout Chambal, there is one thread that ties each of them together—fighting over land. In Mohar Singh's life, too, the struggle began with his effort to save his land and an unsuccessful Mohar was lost in the ravines of Chambal forever.

There was a small white temple in the middle of thorny bushes. 70 years back, there used to be a happy village near this place. Today that village has shifted almost a kilometre away and its original space has been usurped by the Besuli river. Mohar Singh's life as a *baghi* took off from this village. He was a small farmer, who could just manage a decent life. But the history of Chambal says that land here yields not just crops, but enmities too. A quarrel ensued regarding ownership of Mohar Singh's land and a part of his land was forcibly taken over by another family of that village. That added fuel to fire and the case was taken to the police. But during those days, Chambal's police always supported the wealthy. In the case that followed, Mohar Singh became the prime witness. And in Chambal becoming a witness meant to incur even more enemies. One day Mohar Singh's enemies caught hold of him in Jatpura village and kept on forcing him to withdraw his name as witness. But being a wrestler who kept his body well in shape and strength, Mohar Singh did not pay heed to their threats. Then they surrounded him and almost beat him to death. Injured Mohar Singh contacted the police but there too instead of listening to his complaints, the police filed a case against him. Insulted and helpless, Mohar Singh chose the *beehed*. Before jumping into the *beehed*, Mohar Singh went to that temple and promised to destroy his enemies completely. His first target was his enemy. And after that, he kept wandering from one jungle to another in the *beehed*. Initially, he tried to become a member of one of the existing gangs of *baghis* but he was not very successful in his endeavours. Then he decided to form a gang of his own, a gang that later went on to become a synonym of fear in Chambal. To fight a powerful opponent in the village, neither law, nor religion, nor court comes to help. So, the easiest way of gaining power in Chambal was to wait in the forests of Dang and train one's gun upon their enemies. Mohar Singh's gun started firing and one enemy after another fell. Soon after, he started organising small robberies with his gang. That was the beginning of cases against him in police records.

After meeting Mohar Singh, I went to the Mehegaon police station to check their records, I saw that the first case filed against Mohar Singh was registered as case number 140/60. In 1960, the second criminal case was filed against him and his gang in Gouhad police station. And there only the first case of murder too was filed against him in 1961. That was the beginning of a series of killings. Mohar Singh started operating in Bhind and its adjacent areas. But slowly, as his band started growing in number, his area of operation started increasing. He was very stern regarding discipline and order in his gang. Police kept on finishing one gang after the other in Chambal but Mohar Singh's band kept on increasing in size. Mohar Singh had found a way to save his group from the police. He let out a warning that whoever would report to the police against him or his men, his entire family would be wiped out. But it was not just an empty threat, he also started acting accordingly. Mohar Singh's cruelty knew no bounds. Like an ace hunter, Mohar Singh used to swoop down upon the informer and his family and kill each one of them. Most of the cases that were registered against Mohar Singh during this period had to do with the killings of informers and their families. Whomsoever Mohar Singh doubted to be an informer, he would kill the person and his entire family. As a result, Mohar Singh's terror kept on increasing for both police and its informers. And Mohar was reaping its rewards. He became notorious throughout Madhya Pradesh, Uttar Pradesh, and Rajasthan. While the other gangs could not enter their villages for fear of the informers, Mohar Singh and his men stayed in their villages without any fear and could escape even before the police came to know of them.

Mohar Singh had formulated some very stern laws for his gang to follow. One of its chief precepts was that there won't be any female dacoit in the group. Along with it, the group members were strictly forbidden to even raise eyes towards women. Anyone behaving contrary to that would be punished by Mohar Singh himself. And the punishment for such an offence was death. Even today the police praise Mohar Singh in this regard. Even after almost 50 years, Mohar Singh still goes by that diktat. He proudly said, 'No one could ever file a case of eve-teasing or molestation against me or my people.' Between 1960 and 1962, Mohar Singh had established himself as one of the chief leaders of dacoits. Everyday confrontation with the police became routine affair. But Mohar Singh was not bothered with these skirmishes, because as soon as he received money, he procured arms more advanced than those of the police. Also, he kept devising new ways of saving his group from the police. He dared to meet the police head-on, and along with it, his access to advanced arms and ammunition made him the uncrowned emperor of Chambal.

Around this time, Mohar Singh joined hands with other dacoits of Chambal and started a new trend of robbing people and escaping before police arrived. Mohar Singh started operating along with the gangs of Madho Singh, Saru Singh, Ram Lakhan, Master, and Devilal. The police avoided confronting a band of a hundred or two hundred armed dacoits. Mohar Singh's head had become extremely precious for police. Mohar's group would all of a sudden descend upon a village, carry on their lootings and just vanish into thin air. Police informers could never gather any information about their movements. He continued committing major robberies one after the other. The police wanted to stop Mohar, but he seemed to be like the flowing water, completely out of reach. The police started raiding one village after another in search of Mohar Singh, but each time they had to return empty-handed. The dacoits of Chambal had established a kingdom of their own. But the police continued to bring an end to the other major gangs of Chambal.

In 1965 an unprecedented event took place in Chambal. No other gang had managed to show such outrageous courage ever. Mohar Singh's companion Nathu Singh (I later met Nathu Singh who also narrated this story to me) made a plan which even the dacoit leader liked. No one in Chambal had ever thought that they could kidnap someone from Delhi. Let's hear the next part of the story in Mohar Singh's words:

'In Delhi, there was a smuggler of antique statues called Sharma (I don't remember his full name anymore). I had heard that he could go to any place to buy a statue. The entire planning started from here. Someone from the gang informed Sharma that some antique statues had been stolen and those were with a person in Chambal. The smuggler believed in this information and at first sent one of his aides there. We kidnapped that person and made him send a message to Sharma that the information was correct. When Mr. Sharma flew to Gwalior from Delhi, my men brought him to Dang on the pretext of showing the idol. When he saw himself surrounded by my men in the forest of Chambal, he realised that he had fallen prey to dacoits. At that time Sharma had contacts with most of the important leaders and ministers in Delhi. As a result, his disappearance ruffled feathers of the Delhi government. News reached from Delhi to Bhopal. Morena police also received directives from the Centre regarding quick resolution of this matter. But the police did not even get a whiff of Sharma. His family had to finally pay the ransom to get him back. That was till then the highest ransom ever paid in the history of Chambal.' I interrupted Mohar Singh at this point to ask him how much money they could get out of Sharma. The old man laughed through his bushy moustache and said, 'Make a guess.' When I suggested around two to three lakhs, he shook his head. After some more guesses, I accepted defeat. Mohar Singh kept laughing as he narrated the entire story. 'In police records, the amount mentioned is five lakhs. In the history of Chambal, it was till then the highest ransom amount. But I am old now, almost at the door of death. I want to tell the truth now. You are of my grandson's age, so I shall tell you the actual amount. In reality, the amount was 26 lakhs! Sharma's family would have landed themselves in a big soup had they revealed the actual amount to the media. So those buggers mentioned a lesser amount.'

Just listening to the sum made me dizzy. In the police stations around the Chambal area, Mohar Singh became such a name that the police started referring to him as the living ghost. Whenever there was any big crime, the police suspected Mohar Singh's involvement in it. According to an ex-police official, the hide and seek between the police and

Mohar Singh's band often turned funny. But thereafter came a new phase. Though the ruler of Chambal was not an educated person, he was aware that a bullet would only lead to another bullet. That Mohar Singh who had become the terror of Chambal at the age of 28, started seeing shadows of death hovering around himself. He did not leave any stone unturned to get rid of those shadows of death. And then when an opportunity presented itself, Mohar did not let it go. Yesterday's dacoit *Sardar* and today's social worker Mohar has seen many ups and downs in life. In Chambal, Mohar Singh and Madho Singh's friendship is exemplary. Even in the police records, they are mentioned as friends—that is enemy number 1 and enemy number 2. They had the two largest gangs in Chambal. These two gangs of dacoits not only made the people quake in fear but also shook the government. Due to time constraints, I could not visit Rajasthan, but the number of cases against Mohar Singh in police stations I visited in Uttar Pradesh and Madhya Pradesh were enough to place him in the Guinness book of records. Just one of their tables will be enough to illustrate that:

1965 151 robberies, 46 murders, and 114 kidnappings
1966 102 robberies, 40 murders, and 125 kidnappings
1967 90 robberies, 63 murders, and 105 kidnappings
1969 there were around 80 people killed and more than 200 kidnapped

Finally, too troubled with Mohar Singh's activities, Madhya Pradesh government created a one-person commission. The police came under a lot of pressure. There were a series of confrontations. Mohar Singh said that in his 14 years of life as a *baghi*, he had confronted the police approximately 88 times. But each time he could manage an escape. Yet Mohar Singh knew that the police were closing in, and the hide and seek that they were playing in the ravines of the *beehed* could snatch his life away any day. At a time when Mohar was pondering over such things, Madho Singh came to him with a surprise. The latter said that Jayprakash Narayan was making arrangements so that the dacoits lay down arms in his presence. Madho could convince Mohar, and the dacoit chief then decided to leave this life of bullets and cruelty. The dam in Joura in Madhya Pradesh stands as the witness to the highest number of surrenders ever. After serving his term in jail, Mohar Singh returned to Mehegaon. But people remember him even today. He was feared, not just within Chambal, but in the entire country and the highest prize money was also on his head. According to Mohar, 'That I am still alive today, or the fact that no one from my gang became a prey to police bullets, is because neither my gang members, nor I have ever harassed a woman. There was a diktat for my gang members that if ever anybody had anything to do with women, he would be shot to death. This is also the reason why my name is still respected in society.' I could now understand the kind of power he wielded, his extreme courage in those days, which had earned him the epithet of *akru dabangg* in Chambal. I got goosebumps as I listened to his story. He said, 'After the surrender, hundreds of *baghis* including Madho Singh, Nathu Singh, and Saru Singh were taken to the Gwalior jail. The court was set up in the jail itself. I stayed there for 15 months. After that, I spent eight more months in Narsinghgarh prison and then in Mugawali open prison. When we were being transported to the jail after the surrender, there were about 50 to 60 police vehicles ahead and behind us. Finally, the police were giving us a special reception—if not within *beehed*, at least outside it. Within the prison, we used to create so much ruckus that they used to keep a provision of mutton, chicken, and *desi ghee* for us. I remember that the court in the prison had sentenced me to be hanged till death along with a penalty of 10,000 rupees. I found the decision quite ridiculous. I stood up and asked the court that if I am hanged, who is going to pay the penalty of 10,000 rupees?

My family won't be able to arrange that much amount of money. There was a pin drop silence in court after this.' Mohar Singh kept on narrating anecdotes from his life and I could visualise them like cinema. He said, 'After surrendering, one day the SP or deputy SP of Murena district came to Gwalior jail. There, seeing me stand near the prison door, he said, "Mohar Singh if only I could get eight to 10 days more, I would have either killed you or arrested you." I immediately challenged that man there, "What's the problem now? Come on, kill me in an encounter here! When I was outside the jail, we have had hundreds of face-offs but you were pining to get a glimpse of Mohar Singh's face. And now that I have surrendered, like a coward, you are threatening me here!"'

I marvelled at his courage. Had there been a secret encounter inside the jail, no one would have ever come to know of it. In such a situation even the hardest of criminals would be in sweat, and here Mohar Singh threw a direct challenge to the police superintendent. This incident was later used in the movie *Kalia* in a scene where Pran and Amitabh Bachchan were duelling with words inside prison. But Mohar Singh had not just challenged the SP, he had also beaten up a constable inside the jail once. Let us listen to this story in his own words:

'One of the superintendents had created such a situation that all of us (dacoits) gave him a thrashing inside the jail. This news spread so fast that it even reached the ears of the Chief Minister of Madhya Pradesh. Then the Chief Minister spoke to prison staff, "They are all dangerous *baghis* who have just recently come out of the jungles into this jail. If you deal with them patiently, they will slowly change their behaviour."' Mohar Singh added, 'I have no regrets for the murders that I have committed. Many cases have not even been registered by the police to show a reduced crime rate in the state. I had committed around 400 murders. There were 550 cases against my name. But now I pass my life as a farmer and sing *bhajans* or devotional songs in temples in my pastime. I am quite popular as a *bhajan* singer. You can find me wherever there is a *puja* or *bhajan* in the village.'

He had left the life of a dacoit in 1972, but even after that he did not stop murdering. In 2012 he killed his wife and their 15-year-old daughter and threw the bodies in the river because he had doubts about the characters of his wife and daughter. In 2006 he had been sent to jail once again regarding an abduction in Dantiya district of Madhya Pradesh. When he was released in 2012, he went to his wife's parents' place and brought his wife Ramavati Devi and their daughters Arati and Poonam home, on the pretext of his daughter's wedding. Since then, his wife and elder daughter went missing. In June 2012, when police came to interrogate Mohar Singh regarding the double murder case, he confessed his crimes. But no charges could be proved against him as the corpses or their remains could not be recovered in spite of a thorough search in the Sindh river. Always a straightforward person, Mohar Singh did not even accept Phoolan Devi as a *baghi*. Mohar Singh's words might evoke discontentment among feminists, but according to him, it was the media who had created a dacoit out of her. He said, firstly, Phoolan was a woman, and secondly, she belonged to the lower caste. How could a woman become a *baghi*! I persisted, 'But what will you say about the Behemai episode? That was not a lie, was it? She had killed around 21 men belonging to the Thakur clan, by making them stand in a row!' Mohar Singh Gujjar interrupted, 'People write what they wish. But Phoolan was no *baghi*. She was a woman from the Mallar community. In the initial days, she had come to me too, to join my gang, but I had chased her away. Later I heard that she had gone to Malkhan, but was sent away from there as well. *Arre*, how would Phoolan be a *baghi*! She did not even know how to hold a gun; how could she kill a Thakur! Thakurs were killed by the members of her gang and she claimed all the credit!' I could say nothing after this.

Mohar Singh was not just a dacoit, he had also held the post of the chairperson of Mehegaon municipality twice. He thought of joining politics in 1995 and contested the election as an independent candidate supported by the BJP. He had won the election by a huge margin. In 1996 he joined the BJP. That very year he won the election again to become the chairperson of the municipality a second time. And he was an honest chairperson too. Even today, the water tank in Mehegaon, the place where I had got down from the bus, bears proof of his tenure. Today Mehegaon has many *pukka* roads, drainage systems, schools and colleges. But previously this wasn't the picture of Mehegaon city. The architect of this modern Mehegaon was the legendary dacoit Mohar Singh. In his area, he was the much-loved *Baghi-bhai*.

Suddenly a boy rushed up to Mohar Singh and whispered something. Within seconds his eyes turned bloodshot. He looked at me once and said, 'If there's anything more to ask, make it quick. Bholu, take out the gun and load it.' Bholu was Mohar's eldest grandson. I quickly started posing my questions. Bholu returned with a double-barrel gun and sat on the cot trying to put bullets in it. But he could not do so. Mohar lost his patience and shouted at him, 'Motherfucker, you are already 12 and yet don't know how to even hold a gun! Forget about putting bullets in it! Shameless boy! I don't know how you were born in my family! Go and teach that fucker how to do it!' The last sentence was directed towards Mohar's youngest son, the one who had come to give the information.

The 85-year-old Mohar Singh got down from the cot and stood upright. Who would say that just a while ago he was walking with the aid of a stick! He threw away his walking stick and told me, 'Finish your interview in ten minutes, I have to go.' He walked up and down restlessly as he answered my queries. After some time he raised his hand towards me and said, 'That's it. Come again some other time. Your time is up now' and he walked towards the gate where a car was waiting for him. As Mohar Singh sat in the car and it sped towards the enemy, I knew there would not be any mercy for the latter that day. Here follows a part of my conversation with Mohar Singh that day.

Author: Do you repent the crimes that you have once committed?

Mohar: What's the point in repenting after killing someone. And if I had to regret it, then I would not have killed the person. Any feeling of regret should come first. No, I do not repent any of my actions. Yes, I did kill a few people thinking them to be informers of the police but later I found out that they were not so. Some others, who wanted to see the end of their enemies, had given me the wrong information. But even for those, I have no regrets.

A: Did you get any benefit from the government after surrendering?

M: I was given fifteen acres of land.

A: Do you come across your old foes any more?

M: Yes, Rajaram comes at times. But now everybody loves and respects me. In this neighbourhood, everyone calls me *Baghi-bhai.*

A: Did you ever get into problems with other *baghi* gangs during your *baghi* days?

M: No, that never happened. While moving across the *beehed,* we used to meet each other, ask about each other's well-being and continue on our way.

A: Who killed Phoolan?

M: Her enemies.

A: What is your plan regarding your political career?

M: Nothing. See, I have concluded, in politics there are dacoits even greater than those in Chambal. The list of their crimes is longer than ours. I have been disillusioned by politics. As long as I was there, I wanted to serve people and I did so too.

A: Which party do you support now?

M: I do not know whether I support it or not, but I cast my vote for the Congress Party.

A: During your *baghi* days what were your sources for procuring weapons?

M: This I shall not answer. I have never answered this question and will never do so.

A: What do you think you still have to get from life?

M: I have faced many losses, have gained much too. Recently I have bought a tractor. If you want to be respected in Chambal, three things are a must—rifle, tractor, and large moustache. I have all three.

I walked back to the main road. There was still some time left so I decided to walk around in the bazaar, just in case some interesting information came along my way. I was hungry too. I had received royal hospitality from the previous two dacoits, but here I did not receive anything more than a glass of water. So, I went in search of a place to eat. Along the way, I came across Mehegaon municipality. Just beside that was a primary school. I saw the founder's name written on a big hoarding—Respected Chairman—Mohar Singh. Just opposite to the school was a tea shop. The only food available all around was chop, *samosa,* and bread *pakoda*. I had tea and chop and left the place. There was no point in going to the municipality, so I walked a bit further and found my desired destination—Mehegaon police station. I entered the area and was looking around for someone to talk to when a policeman came up to me and asked my requirement. He took me to SI Ranavir Singh Yadav. I asked him about the current situation of Chambal. The account that he gave me was similar to what I had collected from various police stations in Uttar Pradesh;

that there were no more dacoits left in Chambal, that they had solved that problem. But that was just half-truth. Yes, indeed, Chambal does not have as many dacoits as it used to and the terror is also much less. Roadways have improved, cinema halls and shopping complexes have come up in every district. Large departmental stores have come up as well. But it is not true that there are no more dacoits. Yesterday night had proved that to me. I had spent the whole night in the den of a gang of dacoits. I was amused by the SI's words. Who then were Babuli and Gauri Jatav? The ones who were now there, were not *baghis*; their names were not registered in police records, hence the police did not acknowledge their existence. But according to my research, even now around 20 dacoit gangs are operating in Chambal. I asked him if I could check their old records. That would help me in my work. I told him that I would take pictures of those records. He called up someone and after a brief conversation told me that since I have come from such a distance, he would send me to their archive with a constable. He said, 'Please don't write anything that might take away my job. I hope you do understand, after all, I am in government service.' I assured him on this regard and went with the constable. He opened a room in which there were files arranged in iron shelves. Who knows for how many years they have remained covered in dust! The accompanying constable asked me if I needed water, tea or anything else. I asked him to get me a cup of tea and a cloth duster. Covering my face with my handkerchief I was all set to face the dust. I moved from one spine-chilling account to another when suddenly my attention was caught by a name—Gabbar Singh! Who was not familiar with this name which evoked the vision of Amjad Khan walking along the hills and bellowing, '*Kitne aadmi the*?' (How many men were there?) Does that mean there was someone by that name? Driven by curiosity I started reading that file. That story took me to a 90-year-old man, Phirelal, in an unknown village called Chhinsaretha in Madhya Pradesh.

SHOLAY'S GABBAR WAS A KID TO THE REAL GABBAR

'*Pachas pachas krosh tak jab koi bachcha rota hain to ma kya kehti hain? Beta so ja nahi to Gabbar aa jayega*' (Around fifty miles, whenever a child cried, its mother said, come on my baby go to sleep, otherwise Gabbar will come). Most of us have memorised this famous dialogue from the movie *Sholay*. Gabbar's laughter on the silver screen can scare a person to death even today. He began a new era of terror in movies. But did it ever come to your mind that the Gabbar that we watched in the film was a fake? Yes, *Sholay*'s Gabbar was a copy of the real-life Gabbar. The story of Gabbar is one of terror but that terror ends with that of the film. On the other hand, the signs of the real Gabbar can still be found in villages of the *beehed*. Chhinsaretha is just another village among hundreds of others in Chambal. Gabbar's tale was over almost six decades back. But the terror of that tale still runs through these villages. Phirelal—a 90-year-old man was counting his days but he could still remember that day some 61 years back as if it was just yesterday. Only the person who had to spend such a life for 61 years can say how difficult it must have been. Not just Phirelal, there were people in at least a few dozen villages who were nursing Gabbar's wound deep within them. Even today, just the name of Gabbar was enough to evoke some extremely painful memories. You might find his story fictitious and think of him as a villain in movies, but then I must inform you that one of the most successful police officials, IPS K.F. Rustamji, who also finds a mention in the books *Abhisapta Chambal* and *Beehed, Baghi, Bandook*, had considered the news of Gabbar's death to be the best gift. Incidentally, it was the then Prime Minister of India, Jawaharlal Nehru's 70th birthday. Gabbar loved to gift death to people and cut the nose of innocents. By the time Gabbar's story came to an end in Chambal, he was standing on heaps of corpses and rivers of blood. His name had etched dread in the hearts of many. I sat among the cobwebs and dust in that room and revisited the life of Gabbar.

The city of Bhind in Chambal was situated in the middle of the vast expanse of the *beehed*. This city comes up in the lives of most of the dacoits. A few kilometres from Gohad police station in Bhind, a road goes towards the jungle of Dang. The broken road tells a lot about the approaching village. In a village in this area, there is a dilapidated house that had witnessed the greatest terror of Chambal. This was Gabbar Singh's house. Gabbar Singh was born in the village of Gujjars in the year 1926. His father had a small plot of land. In Chambal, the land is the measurement of one's pride. The ones who own smaller areas of land are not much respected in the village. The family had to work as labourers to earn their meals. In this region, even today, stones are chipped away from hills, both legally and illegally. Gabbar's parents worked as coolies to carry these stones. He, too, had to do the same which made him quite strong even as a child. He also sweated himself out in the village *akhada*. Too proud of his strength, he used to challenge villagers to fight with him. From his childhood, Gabbar was a vagabond. He did not have any interest in agricultural work. Once, as a punishment for an offence committed by Gabbar's father, the village *panchayat* had confiscated their small landholding. Soon after this, earning a livelihood became a problem for the vagrant Gabbar. And *the beehed* is just the place for such young men. Thus started his journey to Chambal. He killed a person named Rakhiswar to settle old scores but his life as a dacoit had begun much earlier. In 1940s and 1950s, *baghis* were a terror in Chambal. People respected them out of fear. During that period, Gabbar had gone to meet one of his kin in the neighbouring village, who was also a dacoit. Fascinated by his aura and influence, Gabbar wanted to become a dacoit. When he returned home from his relative's place, Gabbar was a changed person. He kept threatening villagers with death at the drop of a hat.

Meanwhile, Gabbar's father got involved in a dispute in the village and was punished. At the behest of the *panchayat* the family had already lost their right to livelihood within the village. They were socially ostracised. Gabbar then decided to get back his lost prestige in the village. But the path that he chose to regain his honour was gruesome and led directly to the *beehed*. One day Gabbar shot the entire family of Rakhiswar for a petty reason and jumped into the *beehed*. The news that he had killed two people in his very first attempt had reached the *beehed*, so Gabbar could easily gain an entry into the gang of the then famous dacoit, Kalyan Singh Gujjar. It was a belief in Chambal that after committing a murder, one could not turn into a police informer. Hence, to become a gang member or immediately after joining a gang, it was mandatory to commit a murder or loot. Gabbar had crossed the first hurdle easily. To make his mark in the area, he plunged into a series of kidnappings, murders, and robbery. Within a few days of his stay in Chambal, he had started spreading his net of terror all around the area. Madhya Pradesh police started receiving complaints against Gabbar almost daily. Reports of blood-curdling crimes kept on spreading from one police station to the next. Gabbar was one of those very few dacoits in Chambal who did not turn into a dacoit due to circumstances but had voluntarily chosen that life. After his first killings, Gabbar began a game of death with his other existing enemies. Thereafter, he aimed his rifle towards other people in his village. It was his new game, to kill innocent villagers. Gabbar Singh Gujjar unleashed a torrent of death in Chambal. Due to his indiscriminate killings, he also made several enemies within the gang. After a few months, Gabbar selected a few cronies and started a new band of his own. They had already procured arms and ammunitions from the money earned by looting. Henceforth, Gabbar started calling himself the King of Chambal. After every robbery committed by them, his gang members forced the victims to say aloud, '*Chambal Maharaj Gabbar Singh ki jay*!' (Hail the King of Chambal, Gabbar Singh!) Gabbar's band of robbers started committing one crime after another in Bhind, Murena, Gwalior, Dhaulpur, Itawa, and other nearby places. Gradually his gang increased in size which proportionately increased his terror. In the fifties, it was the age of large gangs in Chambal. In such a situation, Gobra or Gabbar became a new problem for the police. He had converted his gang into a machine of death and robbery. Between October and December 1956, there were a few dozen cases, each of murder and loot, filed against Gabbar in Mehegaon police station alone. In other police stations, too, this number was similar, if not more. The police of three states kept on chasing him like a pack of wild dogs. The police were under a lot of pressure to finish off this deadly gang of robbers. But Gabbar was least affected by all this. According to police records, in those few months there were several confrontations between the police and Gabbar's gang, but each time it was policemen who either lost their lives or were gravely injured. Gabbar's gang remained intact and unharmed. All those encounters, from which Gabbar and his band of robbers emerged unscathed, increased his prestige within Chambal. It also boosted his confidence. Like other dacoits in Chambal, Gabbar, too, worshipped the Mother Goddess. He was quite superstitious regarding this matter. Once a week he used to visit the Ratangarh temple of the Goddess, which was built on a hilltop deep within the forest. It was a place very difficult to access even for the police. By the time they reach the spot, Gabbar and his men would escape.

According to the prevalent tradition among dacoits, one day Gabbar announced that he would offer a *nagara* at the temple of Sheetala Devi. At that time this temple was an important site of worship among the dacoits. Gabbar's announcement created a furore in the area because in the past each such incident had led to some fresh crimes by him. One afternoon Gabbar reached the temple with his entire gang. The police were also aware of Gabbar's intention and made plans to catch him. But by the time police surrounded the area, Gabbar and his team were gone. The *nagara* kept in the temple of Sheetala Devi, even today, bears testimony to Gabbar's terror and confidence. That Sheetala temple is almost like a museum of the dacoits because even today it contains many gifts that they had offered to the goddess. The brass lampstand which is lit every evening in front of the deity, was a gift from Putli Bai, the first woman dacoit of Chambal.

As Gabbar had grown from an ordinary criminal to an infamous dacoit, he wanted Chambal to remember him for deeds different from his fellow dacoits. He wanted his name to be synonymous with terror and therefore one day he suddenly took a new decision. That decision had spread his name even beyond Chambal. He decided to punish informers by chopping off parts of their bodies. Gabbar's name echoed through Chambal but Gabbar himself was humming a different tune. Though he had been capable of saving his men from every police encounter, he suspected the villagers to be acting as informers for the police. One afternoon he suddenly arrived at his village, Chhinsaretha. He suspected one of the *chowkidars* of the village to be a police informer. As soon as he entered the village, he and his men caught hold of that *chowkidar* and another villager and dragged them up to the village well. On their way, they picked up two more Dalit men. The terrified villagers were quaking behind the closed doors of their houses. A deathly silence descended over the village. Gabbar kept beating those men mercilessly until they were almost dead. Then in his deep voice, he shouted, 'Come on, give me your nose. Let me see how big it is,' and immediately took out his knife from his waist and chopped off the noses of all four of them. Not stopping at that, he kept firing aimlessly from his gun, shooting the *chowkidar* dead. After this madness, he walked away from there like a king, whistling along his way. Villagers slowly opened their doors but none of them dared to help those dying men and earn the wrath of Gabbar. Somehow the news reached the police in the morning and they reached the spot to take those dying men to the hospital. One among those unfortunate four is alive even now—the 90-year-old Phirelal. He got a new nose at government expense. But just a glance at him was enough to realise how cruelly his nose was cut off. Such an incident of chopping off noses of people from the neighbourhood left people speechless, and in dismay. Though in Chambal there had been some rare precedences of cutting off an enemy's nose, doing this to four people together was unprecedented. It created a new problem for the police and increased Gabbar's terror among villagers manifold. Gabbar, elated at his success, accepted this as his way of punishing villagers at the slightest pretext. If anything irked him, he entered that village to punish the offender in this manner. Old Phirelal still froze thinking of that incident.

Sitting at the village crossroad when you listen to this tale of woe, it will invariably bring to your mind that famous scene from *Sholay* where Gabbar's companion Kalia asks villagers, 'What does Gabbar ask from you villagers, except a handful of grains!' But the people of this village can share real life-tales more gruesome and terrifying than this because they have seen such things happen in front of their eyes. They have somehow been left alive to tell those tales.

In the village crossroad, where we were having the conversation, there were a few other old men along with Phirelal. They said, 'They cut off noses when they did not receive their *galla*, or share of money and fine. *Desi ghee*, milk, rice, and wheat were other things Gabbar expected. Very few people in the village had so much provision to feed a gang of 30. So, after feeding them a couple of times, when the villagers said that there was nothing left with them, Gabbar started terrorising the villagers. At first, he brought two villagers to the middle of the village and chopped off their noses. Then, he kept beating the rest of the villagers with the butt of rifles and sticks until they dropped down unconscious. The villagers were left only when they agreed to pay a fine.' According to Phirelal, in those days, when the daily earning of a labourer used to be around one or two annas, villagers left their village to work in cities for a year to earn an amount of one thousand and one hundred rupees, and they used to pay Gabbar from their meagre earnings.

To add to everyone's woe, Gabbar then came in contact with a tantric in Chambal who told him that if he could chop off noses from 116 people and offer them to Goddess Durga, police bullet won't ever hurt him. And then what was once a hobby for Gabbar turned into his obsession! He became desperate to collect people's noses from villages. He became so obsessed that he had even cut off noses of police constables. Once a policeman had gone to a village to serve a warrant and fell prey to Gabbar. The dacoit cut off his nose too! Soon after, Gabbar chopped noses of 11 people from one village and completed the *puja*. He was particularly angry with the informers. After one face-off with the police, he became suspicious of a group of villagers informing police about his gang's movement. That much was enough for Gabbar. He went to that village, made 21 villagers stand in a row, and shot them dead even before anyone could understand anything. Gabbar's terror intensified further.

The political scenario in Madhya Pradesh got heated up as well. In 1958, the opposition party along with a dozen of Gabbar's victims demonstrated outside the assembly in Bhopal. The Madhya Pradesh government ordered the Inspector General of Police to set up a camp in Bhind to finish Gabbar. The higher officials called a meeting of all police officers in the districts and asked any officer to volunteer to take charge of the mission. The responsibility fell on the young Deputy Superintendent of Police, Rajendraprasad Modi. He had come to limelight after killing the Bandit Beauty, Putli Bai, in a recent encounter. Gabbar became a thorn in Modi's side; such was his terror that people refused to even utter his name, much less provide any information about him. All the efforts made by the police were just going down the drain. Even after two whole years, the police could not get any lead regarding Gabbar's whereabouts. At that time all the three states had separately declared huge prize money on Gabbar's head. But for people in the valley of Chambal, more than the temptation of prize money, saving their lives was more important. Around that time, a humanitarian act by Modi opened a route to reach Gabbar.

A hut had caught fire in the Ghumkapura village near Gohad. Modi reached that place immediately. The police could bring the fire under control but before it was fully extinguished, people suddenly became aware that a five-year-old child was missing and was probably trapped in that blazing hut. Before anyone could react, Modi himself entered that burning hut and rescued the child who was severely burnt by then. DSP Modi gave some money to the child's father, Ramcharan, and urgently sent them off to the hospital in his jeep. The Gohad Police station and the Dang forest were not too far from the village. But the distance between Gabbar in Dang and the police in Gohad was so great that police bullets never reached the dacoit. In such a situation, five days after that fire accident, Ramcharan appeared at the Gohad police station and told Modi that he wanted to repay his debt by helping Modi earn a medal for his service. A surprised Modi could not comprehend Ramcharan's meaning when the man suddenly blurted out that he wanted to provide Modi with Gabbar's address. Ramcharan asked Modi to accompany him to Dang that night. On reaching there, Ramcharan took Modi to the highway and from there to Ghumkapura village. He showed Modi a space between the Bhind highway and Ghumkapura, which was a frequent haunt of Gabbar. Modi himself planned the operation and a trap was laid. After that, it was a wait for the prey.

On 13th November 1959, Modi was surprised to receive a visitor even before daybreak—Ramcharan. He used sign language to inform Modi, in a station full of policemen, that the entire gang had reached that place in Dang. Modi took him aside and gathered all the details. If even a single member of the gang escaped alive, he would kill all the members of the informer's family. Within 10 am, 300 armed police reached Gohad police station. They planned to surround the area from three sides and close in from the fourth. None of the policemen had any inkling of their target or their site of action until very last. From the direction of the highway, Modi and 30 other policemen started moving ahead to close in upon the prey. On another side, Deputy SP Madho Singh had deployed his troops. When they advanced a bit more, they could see Gabbar's men trying to escape from that area by crawling on the ground, moving in a different direction. But there were policemen even on that side. Finally, Gabbar's men started firing. About 11 men kept on firing with all their might. The confrontation had begun at 10 am. From whichever side the dacoits tried to escape, they had to face heavy firing from the police. Slowly darkness was setting in, but the encounter was not yet over. The dacoits could take advantage of the darkness to escape from there, but Modi did not want to let go of the chance to finish Gabbar. So, he took a bold decision, and commanded his companions to launch a direct attack on Gabbar. Anyone willing to be a part of the mission could accompany him. On listening to his words, 11 Gorkha policemen volunteered. They were also a part of the team that had killed Putli Bai. Modi started advancing towards the pit but once again there was heavy firing from the dacoits. Modi charged a hand grenade into the pit. Some dacoits died and as a result, firing was reduced. Even then, as soon as Modi and his men tried advancing, a Mark 3 rifle roared from the other side. Modi threw two more light grenades into the pit and started firing with machine guns. After some time, when the police finally reached the pit, they found Gabbar among the dead dacoits, gasping for his last breath. His lower jaw had been blown off by a grenade. When the search was over, they found that the entire gang had been wiped off. During the time of the operation, Gabbar's men were holding four civilians hostages. In the encounter, unfortunately, two of them lost their lives.

As soon as the news of Gabbar's death was confirmed and announced, thousands of villagers, waiting near the highway, broke into celebration. That encounter brought an end to the most barbaric and hated dacoit of Chambal, the one who had chopped off noses of over a hundred people! But it was certainly not the end of dacoits of Chambal.

Stunned, I sat quietly for some time. I had already taken down the names and addresses of a few of the victims of Gabbar. The place was not too far—just 15 minutes from my location, Chinsaretha. If I left immediately, I could return to Bhind by evening. I did not even know whether the people whose names I had taken down from the police report were still alive. But I was buoyed by my good fortune in Chambal till that point in time and hence wanted to try once. I went back to Ranvir Singh and asked him the way to Chinsaretha.

He said, 'O *Bangali babu*, what will you gain by digging up the past, that too after 61 years!' I tried to explain to Ranvir that I was not going there to gain anything. 'I want to take a look around that place, understand its surroundings, and if there are any survivors who had seen Gabbar with their own eyes, I want to hear their experiences directly from them. If nothing else, at least I shall be seeing a new place, that is also a big thing! And if I can find anything relevant to my work, that will be a bonus. Can you please tell me how I can reach the place?' Ranvir Singh arranged for a jeep to take me there. It would take me to Chinsaretha and drop me back at my hotel later. He would charge me 300 rupees for that. I agreed to the arrangement. The jeep sped across the highway. No, Chambal did not disappoint me even this time. I met the 90-year-old Phirelal within the precincts of the village. In my 15 days of Chambal tour, wherever I have gone, whether it be Madhya Pradesh or Uttar Pradesh, Chambal has been very generous to me. It gave me countless tales, hundreds of life stories, and some great friends—Mahavir Singh, Jagrup Ji, Babuli—Gauri, and here, Phirelal. I am not in touch with them anymore. Though I have the phone numbers of some, I haven't managed to stay in touch. Still, the love and hospitality that I have received from them, the way they had unhesitatingly shared their life stories with me, are experiences that will stay with me till death. Phirelal, Ratanpal, and others in Chinsaretha also told me stories of Gabbar's infernal atrocities. They were all aged between 80 and 90 years. And each of them was a burning example of Gabbar's tortures. As Phirelal said, 'My pain had never subsided *saheb*, but the day the police killed Gabbar, my heart was calmed. It did not reduce my sorrow, but it was like a balm on my ache.'

Sholay is one of my favourite movies. But now, whenever I watch *Sholay*, I see not Amjad Khan as Gabbar, but the face of the Gabbar who remains enclosed in police files of Mehegaon police station. *Sholay*'s Gabbar, in spite of the differences, is loosely based on the life of its real namesake. There is an interesting story behind Gabbar becoming a celluloid character. Salim Khan of Salim-Javed fame, the eminent scriptwriter duo of Mumbai film industry, and the father of Salman Khan, the actor, was the son of Abdul Rashid Khan, a Deputy Inspector General of Police in Madhya Pradesh. The Inspector-General had been directed by the Central government to set up a police camp in Chambal to catch Gabbar. Abdul Rashid Khan was also present in that meeting. He was also present in the team which finally eliminated Gabbar. So, Salim Khan was aware of Gabbar's story. So, when he wrote *Sholay*, he could bring out the brutality of Gabbar to a large extent. There was another Gabbar in Chambal whose actual name was Pritam Singh. His gang operated in the region around Lalitpura in Uttar Pradesh. After watching the movie *Sholay*, Pritam Singh took up the name of Gabbar Singh. I went around Chinsaretha, listened to the stories of village elders, and then returned to Bhind by the jeep. Getting down at the bus stop I went to meet Jagrup-ji and tell him my experiences and stories of Mohar Singh and Gabbar Singh. I had tea with him and then returned to my room in the hotel. I did not have any other place to visit immediately, and wanted to rest.

Bilao is a small village in Bhind. I travelled about 15 kilometres from Bhind bus stand to reach Bilao. The bus that I took early in the morning dropped me on the highway. I crossed the road and took a narrow, unpaved lane just opposite to it. I kept walking along the lane of red soil, with *beehed* and farmlands on either side. Walking for almost 25 minutes I was extremely thirsty but there was no source of drinking water nearby. I had to rest at intervals under shades of trees. I had no idea how long I had to walk to reach the village. Once in a while, some motorcycles passed by. I stopped one of them to ask how far the village was. 'It is just nearby'—was the response. Every motorcyclists I stopped gave the same reply. But the road did not end even after half an hour. My throat was completely parched. After a while I was so irritated that I started singing a song from a popular Bangla movie, *Marutirtha Hinglaj*, '*Koto dur ar koto dur bolo ma*' (How far, oh, how much further, tell me, oh Mother!). All the bikes were coming from the village but none went in that direction that I could ask for a ride.

Finally, I saw a village woman gathering twigs from the nearby jungle and asked her for some water to drink. Initially, she did not want to speak at all. After a lot of effort, I could make her understand that I was coming from a distance and wanted to reach Bilao, and that I was extremely thirsty and was looking for some drinking water. The woman took me to a place behind the farm, to the pump-house, and pointed at an uncovered water tank. On approaching it, what I saw made me stare at the woman in complete bewilderment. There was a layer of moss over the water that had turned black. Numerous insects crawled in it. I asked her, 'How can I drink this water?' She replied, 'This is what we drink.' I continued, 'But this water is so dirty!' The woman then replied, 'There is a water tap around one and a half kilometres from here. But that belongs to the Thakurs. We, the lower caste people, do not have access to it.' There were similar tanks at some distance in the fields. These people had to drink water from there. She said, 'Drink if you want to, or else let me go. I have a lot of work.' Saying so, she immediately balanced the bundle of twigs and branches on her head and started walking. What could I do but follow her! On our way, I came to know from her that Bilao was still quite a distance ahead. Motorbikes kept speeding across us, covering us in ochre dust from the roads. I also came to know that there were around 30 Dalit families in the village. The rest of them were Thakurs, Jaats, and Gujjars. These Dalit families occupied one corner of the village. On days they woke up early and could go to a village well, someone gave them water. Otherwise, once a week they walked around 30 to 40 kilometres to reach Chambal river and brought water from there. They tried to make that water last for three or four days.

Though I could see a well in almost every house, these people had to face such hardships for water. No one would give them water even if they are dying. Is this my India? Even in the 20th century, in spite of having water near their houses, some people had to either walk miles to procure water or drink insect-infested dirty water, simply because of the caste system. What a difference between urban spaces with bright shopping malls and this rural India! I had previously come across blatant casteism in villages of Bankura and Purulia too, but it was not to such an extent. Here people can kill for the sake of drinking water. If someone touches the well of an upper caste person, a *khap panchayat* will decide upon the matter. In front of the whole village, the village elders or the *sarpanch* will give order to take away land from the unfortunate person. He might even be fined. And if the person fails to pay penalty, the women of his family will be raped by upper-caste men. Then they do not lose their caste by touching a Dalit women!

Then one day, one of the unfortunate downtrodden person will break free, and unable to take any more torture, would take up arms and jump in the *beehed*.

I was tired after walking for just 40 minutes while this was their everyday life. My head was bowed down in shame. I could not speak at all and wished to run away from there. Soon there was an opportunity to escape. A motorbike was coming from the highway towards the village. As I waved my hand, a boy of 22 or 23 years stopped near me. I told him my identity and purpose and asked if he could drop me somewhere near the village. He agreed. Dust from the speeding bike hid the darkness of casteism and took me towards another darkness.

The boy said that Malkhan Singh's house was a five minutes' walk to the right from where he dropped me. I followed his direction. There was a large temple atop a *beehed*. Keeping it to my left, I kept walking and reached another small temple. Just to its right was a house with an iron gate. One side of the house had been recently renovated. 'Bagi Samrat Dadda Malkhan Singh'—this was the inscription on the brass nameplate on the door. Just outside the house, a few boys of 17 or 18 years were talking among themselves. Around them, there were a few elderly people too. After introducing myself, I told them that I wanted to meet Malkhan. One of the elders rebuked, 'Say *Dadda*, not Malkhan! You must show him respect.' I expressed my regret, accepted my mistake, and told them that I was a journalist. This time they were more complying. The boys told me that Malkhan did not stay there but visited the place occasionally. They volunteered to take me around the place on the condition that I will shoot their pictures. They also asked me to tell them the name of the TV channel where it would be shown. For them, journalists meant TV reporters! One of the boys said that they were first going to show me the path through which Malkhan had escaped to become a *baghi*. And later they would take me to the temple which had caused Malkhan to turn into a *baghi*. The boys took me to the back of the house. There too was a similar iron gate. I peeped through the gate and saw a room in shambles on one side and a paved courtyard on the other. The house was white. By the standards of the village, it was almost a palace. Behind the house, there was a hut made of mud and leaves. A woman was sitting in the courtyard, occupied with something. I asked her for some water to drink. The boys asked me not to accept water from her as she was a Dalit. I stopped them midway and said, 'I will drink water here only. I do not believe in the caste system.' The boys, stunned, stared at me. The woman too got up by then and was looking at me in bewilderment. I told her, 'Maa-ji, I am very thirsty. Please give me some water.' The woman remained rooted, her eyes wide in disbelief. After a long time, she replied, 'Do not drink water at our place, son. We are low caste people.' I comforted her and once again asked for water. Her face brightened up. She shouted out to someone, 'Hey girl, bring water in the new tumbler and also get some *batasha*. We have a guest at home, so be fast.' A girl of 16 or 17 came out of the room, looked at me, and ran inside. After a while, she brought a brass tumbler full of water and some *batasha* on another plate. I had two of those and then drank the water. The old woman introduced the girl as her daughter-in-law and said, 'My son, you have shown a lot of respect towards us. We have cooked *saag* today. Please have your meal with us. I shall feel even more honoured.' I told her that I was not hungry and I had a lot of work as well after which I needed to return. I promised to have a meal at her place if I ever visited Bilao again. I bent down to seek her blessings. She jumped up and hastily retreated, '*Arre*, what are you doing son! This is sin! May God give you a long life.' One of the boys blurted, 'This is wrong! The whole village will come to know that you drank water at a Dalit's place and you will face problems in getting your work done.' My rebuke stopped him from saying anything further, 'Why don't you just mind your own business and let me mind mine.' The boy only said, 'If you face any problem later, don't complain to me.'

After a few more steps the boys helped me climb to the top of a *beehed*. It was hardly at a distance of 20 feet from Malkhan's back-door. They pointed at an uneven road through the *beehed* and identified it as the road which Dadda had used to escape. When I expressed my wish to follow the road to its end, they said, 'Bhai, this is a very long road and stretches till Bhind.' I insisted, 'Let us at least see as much as we can.' I got down from the *beehed*. The road was just enough for one person to somehow pass, and was full of thorny bushes. As I walked, I had to keep stepping to the right and left to avoid potholes. The lanes gave way to bylanes and blind alleys and finally led into a tunnel. Just above, there was an entire *beehed* and no one could make out the existence of a tunnel from there. As I stood hesitating whether to enter or not, one of the boys suggested that we go in to see. The tunnel took me to a huge hall that could accommodate around 500 people. One of the boys said the *beehed* was full of such tunnels. The dacoits used these tunnels to hide as well as to save themselves from heat and rain. I wondered how many such tunnels had been used as their armoury. Locating these tunnels would be impossible for not only the police, but also the military. I crossed the tunnel to reach another narrow lane and advanced a little more. When I turned around, I could not see the boys. Where did they disappear! I walked back to find them but could not see anyone. I started calling out loudly. My words echoed in the *beehed* but no one replied. Scared, I went back to the tunnel. No one was there too. I was mad with fear by then. I followed the road that I had taken. Moving right and left I once again reached that same tunnel. I ran backward. But no matter whichever lane I took, I always reached the same tunnel. Tension, fear, and tiredness parched my throat. Twice I failed in my attempt to run away from that place, and was left covered in dust. I was so scared that I felt like crying. I sat down in front of that tunnel, took out my phone to see if I could call anyone. But there was no network. I slumped down, tired and dejected. I do not remember how much time had passed but after some time I could hear voices. I rushed in that direction and saw those boys. They had brought some more people with them. As soon as they saw me, they rushed forward and pelted me with questions—where did you go despite our warnings, do you know how long we had been searching for you, and so on. I was in a bad state by then. I just somehow managed to ask them to take me away from that place. With much difficulty, I came out from the maze that the *beehed* is.

Once again, I reached Malkhan's house. Those people took me to the temple there. The land on which that temple had been built was the root cause behind Malkhan becoming a *baghi*. I was sitting in a courtyard in front of the temple. I had drunk water at a Dalit's house—so I was not allowed inside the temple. Villagers brought me water in an earthen pitcher as they would not let me touch any of their vessels. The old woman, at whose house I drank water, rushed to see me. She said, 'Come with me to my house to take some rest. These people will neither let you enter the temple nor take you to their home. You will fall sick sitting in the sun here.' I accompanied the woman to her place. She wiped the dust from my body using a *gamcha*. And made me sit on her bed. I rested there for about 15 minutes. She gave me a bottle of water and said, 'Keep it with you, for the journey.' After that, I started taking a walk around the village but no one talked to me properly as I had drunk water in the house of a lower caste woman. I went to that police station that had been built in the village to arrest Malkhan Singh. Now, only its ruins remained on top of a *beehed*. I climbed up another *beehed* to take its pictures. But my regular digital camera was not equipped to capture that picture properly. The *beehed* was not high enough to offer me a good view or take the picture. I went to a couple of houses, requesting them to let me climb to their roof to click better pictures of the police station but they would not let me in. I would pollute their house by stepping in. One of them even pointed at a tower at a distance and suggested I could climb that if I needed an altitude. I realised I would not be getting any more help from this place and started my journey back. I bade farewell to the village of Malkhan Singh, the Baghi emperor, Dadda Mallkhan Singh. There was a time when his name evoked terror. He had picked up a fight with the village elders to retrieve the temple land. I was walking along the roads of that Malkhan Singh's village.

DADDA MALKHAN SINGH

Six feet height, a large moustache, clad in khaki uniform, American self-loading rifle in one hand and loudspeaker in the other—for years, this was the appearance of Malkhan Singh, the terror of Chambal. There were a few hundred cases of kidnapping, looting, robbery, and murder registered against him. But he used to roam about fearlessly in Chambal. Those who thought that Chambal had become peaceful after dacoit leaders like Mohar Singh, Madho Singh, or Pancham Singh had surrendered in front of Vinoba Bhave and Jaiprakash Narayan recognised their mistake quite soon. After the fall of the titans, Chambal or the *beehed,* too, was on the lookout for a new hero. The arrival of Malkhan Singh filled that void. Chambal has always offered refuge to the common man caught in land feuds, stranded between the police and the mercenary. Malkhan's life in the *beehed* too started with his need to save himself from his enemies in the village. Once he took to *beehed*, his terror started spreading quickly. After escaping from police confrontations more than six times, Chambal had accepted Malkhan as its hero. Police kept on pursuing him but they could never lay a finger on him. The hundreds of cases registered against him were still not all the crimes that Malkhan had committed. Many of his victims or their families had not even filed a case against him out of fear. But what is the story behind the transition of Malkhan Singh from the son of a small farmer in the village to the dacoit king of Chambal!

Thousands of houses in the villages of Chambal have their back doors leading to the *beehed*. It is probably an unwritten rule to keep one of the doors in the backs open. Bilao, under Umri police station, is like any other village in Chambal. In that village, there is a white house that still carries the name-plate of 'Baghi Samrat Dadda Malkhan Singh.' Malkhan's ancestral house was a little ahead along the same road. One had to enter the new house to get permission to enter the ancestral one. Even after 50 years, one could see that house, in its dilapidated state, which had once merged itself with Chambal. Fifty years ago, a 17-year-old Malkhan had taken up arms against the village zamindar. Kailash Pandit was the most influential person in the village of Bilao. He was the family priest of the Khangar Thakurs and owned most of the land of the village. He had also retained the post of the village sarpanch for years. Like most of the boys in the village, Malkhan too used to hang around with Kailash but at times he also protested against him openly. That had somehow irked Kailash Pandit. The relationship started deteriorating from that point. Malkhan had no idea of the far-reaching consequences that his actions will cause. The police were hand in glove with Kailash, and under his influence, the police framed a false case against him. He was arrested but got bail within a few days. But those few days had changed Malkhan completely. After that, he started openly questioning the ways of Kailash Pandit in *panchayat* meetings. The main dispute between Kailash and Malkhan revolved around an illegal possession of temple land. There was a hundred-acre of land on the banks of the river Sindh, a tributary of Chambal, upon which the temple was built. Kailash's people had usurped that land and used it for farming. But Malkhan raised the issue in the *pan-*

chayat and wanted that land to be returned to the temple. The already deteriorating relationship turned into bitter enmity over this issue. Kailash Pandit could not digest the idea of returning that piece of land to the temple. He told the police that Malkhan was associated with the gang of the infamous dacoit, Girdariya. He also suggested that the police could finish off the gang with the help of Malkhan. Police once again arrested Malkhan. A helpless Malkhan, to save himself, gave them an address, partly true and partly fabricated. But the police could not catch Girdariya and his team. Provoked by Kailash, the police decided to teach Malkhan a lesson. From then on, Malkhan's life was jeopardised even more.

One day while Malkhan was asleep, there was a raid in his house. The police captured him even before he was fully awake and took him to the police station. There he was beaten black and blue and he lost his ability to even move. Injured Malkhan was further shocked when the police took him from the police station and threw him at Kailash Pandit's feet. The police wanted to kill him, but in front of so many villagers, there was a risk of getting implicated in charge of an encounter. The police, therefore, took him back to the police station. Village politics further aggravated the enmity. The call of the *beehed* was becoming too strong for Malkhan to ignore any longer. In 1970, Malkhan won the village *panchayat* election and hence became a major threat for Kailash Singh. During the sarpanch elections, one of the five village elders—a Dalit and staunch supporter of Kailash Singh, was murdered. The police once again implicated Malkhan and one of his companions in the case. The court sentenced the two of them to life imprisonment. On the other hand, the angry Dalits in the village killed Malkhan's guru, Jagannath alias Hitler, in public view. This incident, which took place in Holi, broke Malkhan completely. Crying upon the dead body of Jagannath, Malkhan took the vow of not playing Holi till he avenged the death of his guru. The law of Chambal—death for death, and that song sung by minstrels in Chambal—'futile is the life of that person whose enemy is alive,' was once again proven true. Malkhan's life was in grave danger. His enemies in the village were baying for his blood. In 1976, one night when he was sleeping, there was heavy firing on his house. Malkhan somehow managed to sneak out of the back door and escape into the *beehed*. Thereafter he accepted the *beehed* as his destiny and decided to confront his decade-old enemies head-on. In the language of Chambal, *usne beehed pakad li* or, he accepted the *beehed*. After a few days, Malkhan suddenly appeared in front of Kailash Singh's house and shouted, 'Save yourself, if you can, Kailash!' He kept on firing from the Sten gun that he was holding. Kailash took three bullets but somehow survived while his companion, shot at multiple times, lost his life.

The police made life difficult for Malkhan and he knew that all roads of returning to society were closed for him. Chambal was his only way out. So, he formed a gang in Chambal. The police named Malkhan and his gang E-49 or enemy number 49. An award of Rs 10,000 was declared upon his head. The village of Bilao was now set to witness a series of enmities. The first person to join Malkhan's gang was one of his distant cousins and friend, Prabhu. They chose kidnapping as means of getting money for arms. Malkhan followed the tradition of the *beehed*—he donated the money earned from his first abduction for the maintenance of the temple. Though Malkhan had left the village, his enemies still wanted him dead. Prabhu was murdered. On the day of his funeral, the police laid a trap to capture Malkhan. But Malkhan managed to escape. Malkhan kept committing one crime after another and the award declared upon his head kept increasing. Within five months, the reward was increased by 5,000 rupees. The police did not let go of any means of apprehending Malkhan. They even sought help from the dreaded dacoit Mohar Singh, promising him extended parole. Though Mohar Singh helped the police, they could not reach Malkhan.

That very year Malkhan killed two Dalit men to avenge the death of his guru. To get rid of Malkhan, the police managed to convert one of the gang members into their informer. But even he was killed by Malkhan. Just as the police were trying their best to catch Malkhan, Malkhan's terror kept on increasing in Chambal. Within a year, Malkhan had raised to the position of E-3 from E-49. Malkhan and his men started abducting. But the gang started splitting up over issues of sharing the ransom money. Five members of his gang left Malkhan. A dacoit named Babu Gujjar also stole his favourite Winchester rifle before running away. Babu Gujjar was the same person who had abducted Phoolan and raped her for days. Later Vikram Mallah killed him to rescue her. Malkhan's gang started focussing more on kidnapping than robberies. They kidnapped people from villages like Lakshmanpur and Barpur and extorted hefty ransoms. Around the same time, Malkhan killed one of his gang members, suspecting him of being an informer. Slowly Malkhan and his group became confident of themselves and began targeting police personnels. Malkhan murdered a constable of the PAC (Provincial Armed Constabulary) and after that, he and his disintegrating gang gathered once more in Chambal. After a gap of six years, they once again extorted a large sum of money by abducting a few more people and celebrated Holi.

From this point, Malkhan started showing his true colours. To assume the title of dacoit king, he did not hesitate to confront the police in face-to-face combats. In the Lalpura *beehed* in Chambal, he had a major confrontation with the police. Even after a shoot-out that lasted for almost 18 hours, his gang had managed to escape from the police. To the dismay of the police, another *baghi*-demon had come to rule in Chambal. Desperate to catch Malkhan, the police forces of Madhya Pradesh and Uttar Pradesh launched a combined attack. But a confident Malkhan did not stop abductions even then. Within a month, he threw a direct challenge to the police by abducting a high-profile person from Silua *ghat*. The police intensified its operation and surrounded him within Chambal. But Malkhan, used his wit to run away with his gang to a forest near Samthar in Jhansi. The police had just one target—Malkhan. Yet Malkhan continued his activities boldly in Chambal. He became such a terror that even his formidable foe was forced to leave the village. Kailash Pandit's family left their village and started living in the city under police protection. That was the period when other gangs were scared of Malkhan too. They tried their best to keep Malkhan in good humour. But Malkhan had not forgotten the traitor Babu Gujjar. One fine day he went to Babu's village and killed his father, uncle, and the uncle's son. Babu was not there. Malkhan kidnapped another brother of Babu and brought him along with himself. Around that time Phoolan Devi and Vikram Mallah earned Malkhan's trust by killing Babu Gujjar and bringing his favourite Winchester rifle back. Though Malkhan did not accept Phoolan's request of making her a part of his gang, he helped her in other ways. As Malkhan's activities started making newspaper headlines, the police felt more pressurized. Once again Uttar Pradesh and Madhya Pradesh police launched a combined operation against Malkhan. But Malkhan managed to escape to Rajasthan. He started kidnapping people even there. This time the police surrounded him in Bharatpur, Rajasthan. But, once again, Malkhan escaped with his gang. As Malkhan's terror increased, so did the pressure on the police to apprehend the *baghi* leader. Around this time once again Malkhan's gang started disintegrating. A few dacoits left his gang to join others. But completely unperturbed by all these, Malkhan continued with his abductions and ransom demands. In no time, Malkhan was being treated as the emperor of Chambal. He killed anyone who went against him. In Bah district, Dadda Malkhan Singh put three dacoits to sleep forever. The situation was such that it seemed Malkhan had his eyes on every street of Chambal. Just within five months, Malkhan committed so many crimes that the police went almost berserk. The list below will testify the facts—

30th October — four persons kidnapped from Osai
22nd December — three people murdered
26th December — a farmer abducted from Gariya
11th March — seven people abducted from Vinatkipura
27th March — five people abducted from Asthpura
3rd May — four people abducted from Nawada
1st June — nine abducted from Tehangur

Malkhan had become an enigma for the police. They further increased the prize money on Malkhan's head to 40,000 rupees. They planned an operation and surrounded Chakranagar to arrest Malkhan and his group but by then the dacoits had gone beyond the reach of the police. Malkhan was like a djinn who could become invisible at any given point. Finally, it was decided that the three police commissioners of the three states would jointly lead an operation to bring an end to Malkhan's tyranny. But whenever the police took a step against Malkhan, he responded with abduction or murder. He earned the epithet of 'the cunning tiger of Chambal.' In spite of all these, the fire of revenge was still blazing in the heart of the dacoit king Malkhan and he was desperate to finish his enemy. The *baghi* Samrat had not forgotten Kailash Pandit. He combed through Chambal to search for him but the police had kept Kailash under impenetrable security in a place in Jalaon district. Malkhan grew restless to take revenge.

In Chambal, Malkhan was known as a dacoit leader with deference. He was the last of those *baghis* in Chambal who lived their lives by their principles. They never did anything which they considered unjust. The following incident is an example of the strong principles that Malkhan had. According to one of the popular stories of Chambal, once some members of his gang kidnapped Kailash Singh's daughter from her village. As soon as Malkhan came to know about the occurrence, he rebuked his whole gang. Then he touched the girl's feet to ask for forgiveness and himself accompanied her back home, loading her with plenty of gifts. It was unbelievable! Malkhan had given an ultimatum to his gang regarding misbehaving with any woman. The only punishment for such an offence was death. Because of this principle, Malkhan gained a heroic stature in his village. Just as Mansingh was popular as Dau, Malkhan too was affectionately referred to as '*dadda*' by his villagers. The man who had embraced *beehed* with the promise of killing Kailash Pandit and taking revenge, finally got his much-awaited news. One of his closest companions, Kashiram Lohar, had shot Kailash Pandit to death with multiple bullets; the latter was then living under the security of Special Armed Police. It was a day of celebration for Malkhan. In his life as a *baghi*, there were more than 400 cases against Malkhan, of which there were 185 murder cases. His revenge was complete. After that Malkhan did not stay in the *beehed* for long. In 1983, he surrendered himself to the law in the presence of the then chief minister, Arjun Singh. He had given the condition that if the government returned the temple land to the temple, only then would he surrender and that it should come in writing from the Prime Minister, Rajiv Gandhi. Only after obtaining written promise from the Prime Minister did Malkhan surrender. By this time, he had lost his first wife and children. After coming out of the *beehed*, he married again at the age of 60.

He had two children now. Similar to the other dacoits who had surrendered, Malkhan too did not live in his village. I did not know his current residence. I was not even sure if I would get to meet him. Malkhan was a legendary figure in Chambal. His respect for women was exemplary. He never allowed any woman to become a part of his gang. After the death of Vikram Mallah, Phoolan Devi was left alone in Chambal. Once during that time, she had come to Malkhan under the recommendation of his nephew, dacoit Ghanshyam Singh alias Mridha. She came to seek help with folded hands. But ignoring the commendations of his nephew, Malkhan had refused help to Phoolan because he did not want to include any woman in his band. But his gang was not completely devoid of women. There was a bandit queen in his group, Kamala Sundari. But she was different from other women robbers because she was not a kept woman of Malkhan. She was known within the gang as Pushpa *behen*, sister of Malkhan Singh. According to police records, Kamala was not actively involved in robberies. She used to kidnap small children. Her task was to look after those children and other members of the gang, attend to Malkhan and cook for the group.

I was walking along the road of Bilao and had almost reached the highway when I heard someone calling from behind, '*Bhaisaab, o bhaisaab*, wait for a minute.' I turned around to see a man of around 45 years following me. He asked, 'Are you a journalist? You want to meet Dadda?' I looked at him with surprise and asked him the reason for his query. That man, Charan Singh Kushawa said he was in touch with Malkhan and had met him a couple of days back at a wedding. Malkhan was staying in Gwalior these days and was a respectable person now. If he accepted an invitation, it raised the status of the host. He gave me his mobile number and asked me to get in touch with him later as he was going to Gwalior that day. He said that he will try to locate Malkhan's current address for me. I said that he could have told me all these things in the village itself. He replied, 'I do not believe in the caste system but I have to live in this village with my family. By helping you, we would have been ostracised by other villagers. That is why I have come this far to give you the information. Please write about this village too. There has been zero progress in this area. Come, I shall show you something.'

He took me to the top of a *beehed* nearby, and pointed at a distance. I saw a crane and other pieces of machinery being used to level a part of one of the *beeheds*. I appreciated and said it was good that they will have more arable land now. I was amazed to hear his reply, 'So even you got fooled by it *patrakar-babu*! This land is not for us. These are for the political leaders and other big shots. They are taking ownership of the *beeheds* one after the other. After that, farmhouses will come up and there will be midnight parties, dancing girls, and unlimited liquor.' He pointed at a similar farmhouse in another direction. I asked him why were they not protesting against these. Charanji laughed at my naivety, '*Sahab*, we are very ordinary people. How much power do we have to go against politicians?' This village does not have enough water, there are no schools. Even the basic requirement for a decent lifestyle was missing. Yet, we hear noises made about cleanliness in villages and various other schemes of the Prime Minister! Progressive India! All those were empty promises, and only for show. In reality, there was nothing. It was all darkness in the interiors of these villages.

I got a bus immediately after reaching the highway, and once again, started my journey towards Bhind. While travelling by bus I kept on musing about my stay in Chambal till now. I have heard so many stories, watched its many faces, had such rich experiences—all seemed to be one long continuous movie on the silver screen. I was meeting the right people at the right time and had no clue how all these were happening. It had begun right after I had reached Agra—meeting Mahavir in Jyot Kalan, coming across Yashvardhan in the jeep, meeting Ravi-ji and Jagrup-ji in Bhind and Charan Singh here in Bilao. Everything appeared to be predestined. Was it even possible to have so many coincidences! But what has amazed me the most abut Chambal is endurance of the local people here. In spite of so much torture, exploitations, injustice, denial for rightful living, they have resigned themselves to their fate. One cannot hear them complaining. Now that Chambal is free from dacoits, their *beeheds* are being taken away, their villages do not have electricity or even a school; even then they are silent. It is not that the government is unaware of their problems. The problem of *baghis* had become such a serious issue in the past that the central government had to keep a close eye on the place. In fact, even now there is a vigilance over Chambal.

There has not been any development even in the villages of Uttar Pradesh, Delhi, and West Bengal but the kind of darkness that exists here is unmatched by any other place in India. Casteism, religious differences, criminal activities, etc are present throughout India. But nowhere did I find such lack of infrastructure and development. I have seen huts and slums in Delhi, West Bengal, and other places but not of this extent. Here, development has been limited to urban areas. In urban language, progress means concrete roads. In my trip across Chambal, I have seen people fuming from within, seething in dissatisfaction. Chambal might have calmed down but it has not changed its character. It can go back to its old ways once again. I could not help but remember Mohar Singh's words. Towards the end of our conversation, he had started addressing me as *beta* and said, 'We had given up arms in the hope of rehabilitation. Some of us have been rehabilitated but most have not.' Whenever he met his old friends, he had heard quite a number of them contemplating taking up arms again. If once again Chambal goes back to its days of terror, it will not be right to blame the people here. Mohar Singh received 150 acres of land from the government, but most of his companions did not get anything. For example, Madho Singh did not receive any aid at all. In his last years, he had to wear tattered clothes and perform magic shows on roads. He did not have food for days and had to satisfy his hunger by drinking water from roadside taps. The government washed its hands off responsibilities after creating newspaper headlines for organising the mass surrendering of dacoits. Whether during Vinoba Bhave's time or Jayprakash Narayan's time, the story has remained the same. 1960, 1972, 1983, and even thereafter, whenever dacoits have laid down their arms, political leaders have thronged the place to share limelight, but no one has worked for their rehabilitation. No steps were taken to prevent them from going back to the *beehed*. According to one of the statistical reports, almost 30 percent of the *baghis* who had surrendered had been forced to return to the *beehed* due to lack of better livelihood. But who is to take responsibility for this? No one so far has.

I reached Bhind and took a rickshaw to Waterbox, to meet the oldest living *baghi* of Chambal, Lokman Dixit. He was the most trusted companion of Mansingh and was affectionately called Lukka Daku. Asking my way from the Waterbox, I reached a two-storeyed house. I could see a few children studying in a room. As soon as I knocked, someone opened the door and asked me my purpose. I identified myself as a journalist and said that I wanted to meet Lokman Dixit. I was not prepared for what I heard next. Just 10 days back Lukka Daku had passed away. He was 96 then. The lady who had opened the door asked me inside and went to call Lukka Daku's grandsons. I sat on a chair and wondered why Jagrup-ji had not told me anything about the death of this legendary dacoit leader who had been in charge of the gang after Mansingh and Rupa Maharaj. He must have heard about it! Or, is it possible that the erstwhile terror of Chambal died in complete oblivion, hidden from everyone's knowledge? He had an amazing personality and his life was no less fascinating. A man not known to ever mince his words had died a quiet death. I regretted not visiting him a few days earlier. I lost a golden opportunity to listen to his experiences in his own words. It is a regret that will remain with me forever.

When a brahmin turns *baghi*, he can either become a

Chanakya or a Lukka Daku. Lokman Dixit alias Lukka Daku had joined Mansingh's group, unable to bear the exploitations of the British and the zamindars any more. They were the first generations of modern dacoits in Chambal. Before Independence, Mansingh and his gang had robbed many English men and zamindars. When India gained independence, they were hopeful of getting justice. But in reality, that did not happen. Hence the gang continued with its old ways. In 1955, Mansingh was killed and after him, Rupa Maharaj too lost his life. Lukka had to take up responsibility of the gang, and very soon he became the terror of Chambal. But not just as a robber. Lukka had other feathers in his cap too. Lukka was one of the key players behind the large number of dacoits laying down their arms in front of Vinoba Bhave in 1960. Later he became popular as Pandit Lokman. But what had caused such a change of heart in this infamous dacoit? His grandson narrated the incident in detail. It had happened at a time when Lukka's name was enough to evoke dread. He was walking along the road of Bhind when he collided with a rickshaw puller. The rickshaw puller did not know him so he got down from his rickshaw, kicked him hard, and rode away on his rickshaw. He could not believe this! The person whose name sent shivers down the spine was kicked by a simple rickshaw puller! This incident completely changed the robber. Lukka was extremely religious and used to read aloud the Ramayan even while in the *beehed*. He thought it to be divine retribution that he was kicked by a rickshaw puller. This incident made him contemplate surrendering to the law. He got in touch with Vinoba Bhave. On 19th May 1960, he along with 11 other dacoits laid down arms at Vinoba Bhave's feet. Life after the *beehed* was quite tragic for Lukka, a dacoit who had once played with numerous lives. His eldest son Satish Dikshit died due to cancer. His younger son Ashok Dikshit was killed in a road accident in Bhind. But the 96-year-old Lukka did not have regrets. Till the last day of his life, he maintained that whenever he had killed some one, he did not think of the victim's family, so, it was just that he too must witness the death of his children. Due to this philosophy of acceptance, the tragedy of losing both his sons did not overwhelm him.

Lukka was the first dacoit to celebrate Independence Day in Chambal. On 15th August 1947, Lukka gathered all the dacoits of Chambal at one place. The national flag was brought. All the dacoit gangs contributed to buying and distributing a few quintals of *laddoos* in the nearby villages. Considering the times, this was quite a remarkable achievement. It is said that Lukka was a close friend of Ram Prasad Bismil and followed his principles. To evade the British, police Ram Prasad Bismil had often sought shelter from Lukka. Though true, it has never been written down anywhere in history. Still, it remains etched in the hearts of those who had witnessed it. I was talking to one of the grandsons of Lukka. He shared another extraordinary anecdote with me. After surrendering when Lukka was produced in court, the judge had asked him about the actual number of murders committed by him. He immediately replied with a counter-question, 'Judge *saab*, do you remember the number of *rotis* that you have eaten?' The judge was shocked to receive such an answer. Towards the end of his life, Lukka used to shut himself up in a room, keeping even lights off. He suffered from a constant fear that friends or family of those he had killed will come to take revenge. He was so scared that he even stopped stepping out of the house. He too did not receive the promised aid from the government. His wife had to work as a primary school teacher to run the family.

I did not stay there long because there was nothing much that I could get. The grandchildren did not know much about his life. Whatever they knew were stories they had heard. Exhausted with the day's event, I started going towards my hotel. I had to face such a horrendous episode in the *beehed*, and then there was the long walk to and from the village. How could my body permit anymore! After taking a shower I began listening to recordings of the past few days and went through my notes. Ram came to see if I needed any tea. He said, 'I know you have come here to work on the *baghis* and have to travel to various places. Drink some tea, you will feel refreshed.' I asked, 'How did you know that I have come to work on the *baghis*?' He replied, 'I know everything. I work in this hotel and keep my eyes and ears open. Moreover, in this area, everyone loves me. You have met Jagrup ji too, see I know everything!' His sleuth-like conversation brought a smile to my lips. I asked him to bring tea and he returned shortly with it. I felt an affection for that boy. 'Do you have time?' I asked him. 'I would like to talk with you'. Ram said he was free at that time because he did not have much to do in the afternoons. There were only very few boarders.

I asked him about his family, his home, and why he was working in a hotel in the city instead of farming? Suddenly the ever-smiling face turned pensive. That young boy, somewhere in his twenties, became silent. I was a bit hesitant to probe further. Yet, after persisting with the same question, he suddenly said, '*Sahab*, at times even I feel like becoming a *baghi*.' I had never expected to hear such a thing from him! When I asked him the reason, he said, 'I have around 8 or 10 bighas of land in the village. But an influential person is wrongly occupying it. My father, unable to bear this grief, has lost his life and I had to leave my village to work here. There are times when I wish to kill that man and take refuge in the *beehed*.' Ram's words reminded me of Baghi Mohar Singh. He had said, 'As long as there is injustice in Chambal, *baghis* will be born.' I was also reminded of Gauri's words—'No one comes to the *beehed* for fun.' I have been at Bhind for the last two days. I interacted with Ram, met various dacoits, and spoke to them. I realised that those dacoits too were in a situation quite similar to that of Ram. They had taken up arms due to the way the rich and powerful exploit locals. Someone's wife or sister has been raped in the fields and when the person went to the police to protest, the police, bribed by the accused, had got that person implicated in false charges. Someone's land has been forcefully occupied, or someone has been forced to the *beehed* due to the envy of friends and kin. Chambal is known for its courage.

If this land has birthed dacoits, it has also birthed soldiers who sacrificed their lives for their country. In many families, it is seen that among the brothers, while one is a fearsome dacoit, the other is a soldier posted at the border. Jayshriram Baghel of Ridauli village in Bhind district was an active member in dacoit leader Vidya Gaderia's gang for six years. His younger brother was a subedar in the army. A powerful man in the village had killed Jayshriram's uncle. He had joined the dacoits to take revenge for his uncle's death. According to the police, *baghis* are treated as heroes in their respective communities and receive special treatment. The police also mentioned that *baghis* in the past had a code of conduct. They were so strict about it that anyone breaking the code was punished by death. But those who become *baghis* now do not care for any principles. They are now professional robbers and have not turned *baghis* to protest themselves from exploitation. They do not murder or loot people like the *baghis* of earlier times. These days, their prime business is abduction. In Chambal, they have elevated abduction to the status of entrepreneurship! It is also a business like any other business. These insights amazed me! The more I heard, the more shocked I was at my ignorance. I did not have much time. So, bidding goodbye to Ram I focussed on my next course of action. I decided to check out from the hotel the next morning, to go to Gwalior. It would be easier if Charan-ji gets me Malkhan's address. Else, I would have to try and find him myself. I went to the reception to inform them that I would be checking out. Then I went to the bus stand to make arrangements for my Gwalior trip.

I woke up early to get ready. Ram brought me tea. I was surprised to see him standing with a long face. I asked, 'What's the matter, Ram?' He replied, 'You are leaving today, but will you remember me? Many boarders come here. They give generous tips if they like my work. But I have never met anyone like you who wanted to know the sorrows of our lives.' I had no reply to this. What could I have said to this boy! After drinking tea, I took my rucksack and came down with Ram. I gave him my business card and asked him to get in touch with me whenever he visited Kolkata. I would never forget him.

I boarded the bus to Gwalior. It was a journey of two or two and a half hours. Bus fare was one hundred and ten rupees. The bus sped through National Highway 719, crossing river, forest, and the *beehed* along its way. I was leaving behind stories of Mahavir Singh, Raviji, Babuli-Gauri, Mohar Singh, Gabbar Singh, in search of newer stories. I had fallen asleep while travelling and woke up only on reaching Gwalior. I found an average hotel near Gwalior station and checked into it. Then I called up Charan-ji of Bilao village. He told me that though he had not been able to procure Malkhan's address, he had received information that the *baghi* was staying at a place called Sadashiv Nagar, behind Gwalior Central Jail. I had to finish my work within a couple of days so there was no time to waste. I immediately left in search of Malkhan. I hired an auto to take me to Sadashiv Nagar. I said I will take a look around the place and return. We made a deal at 400 rupees. The auto sped through the main road of Gwalior. I caught sight of a huge fort upon a hillock on my right as the auto took a right turn. The auto driver informed me that it was the famous Gwalior Fort built by the great Rajput king, Raja Maan Singh. The fort was spread over a large area. As we moved forward after circling the fort, I came across two sparkling malls as well. After quite some time I asked the auto driver how much longer we needed to travel. He parked the auto on the roadside and asked, 'There are two Sadashiv Nagars here. Which one do you want to go to?' That caught me in a fix. Finally, I asked him to take me to Gwalior Central Jail. The auto stopped near the Central Jail.

I asked a few people around but no one could tell me where Sadashiv Nagar was. It was noon so the roads were quite deserted. There were some peddlers with carts. I asked them too but even they did not know. Ultimately, I decided to enter the prison premises in the hope of getting some information. After identifying myself and stating my purpose to the guard stationed outside the prison, I entered the prison complex. It was a huge area. Many people were waiting there to meet their dear ones. Since I could not understand whom to ask, I entered the chamber of an official. Surprised at my request he scoffed, 'Do you think we carry Malkhan's address in our pockets? I don't understand you people.' While he was speaking, a constable entered the room. He told me that there was a Sadashiv Nagar just behind the jail. By then the auto driver had also come to know of my identity and was bubbling with enthusiasm to locate the house of the famous *baghi*, Malkhan Singh. He took up the responsibility of finding the address. Crossing the jail, he kept asking for directions from other auto drivers that he was familiar with and finally reached Sadashiv Nagar. But how should we find the house? We entered the by-lane and moved forward asking people for directions. These lanes and by-lanes reminded me of the streets of Varanasi and the way my auto driver navigated them was thoroughly commendable. A slight mistake could have made him slam the auto against the walls of the houses. After searching for a long time someone directed us to a house which was almost falling apart. There was no plaster on the walls on three sides, but there was a huge gate at the entrance. The driver parked the auto in a space in front of the house and said he would wait for me there.

I rang the calling bell and waited with bated breath. When the person opened the door, I stood gaping at him. A man of extremely dark complexion, with shoulder-length hair, though balding from the front stood in front of me. His large eyes were red but most spectacular was his moustache. The moustache, covering his upper lip, extended up to his ears. And it was shining black. A long red *tilak* marked his forehead. His whole appearance was frightening. It did not need any mentioning that this was Malkhan Singh. But such a scary person asked my purpose of visit in a polite voice. In spite of the politeness, the voice itself was enough to make anyone quake with fear. It took all my courage to somehow utter that I had come from Kolkata to take his interview. Saying, '*Aayiye*, come in,' Dadda Malkha Singh, the last *baghi* with principles, ushered me into his drawing-room. Once Mansingh was famous as Baghi Samrat. And, if there is any true successor of Mansingh, it has to be Malkhan Singh—so strong were his ideologies.

Entering the drawing-room, he sat upon a bench beside which there were two chairs. He called out aloud to someone inside for tea and savouries. His booming voice almost robbed me of mine. He inquired, 'Where did you get my address?' I said that I had to ask around a lot to reach him. When I told him that I had been to his ancestral house in Bilao, he smiled. A little boy brought a cup of tea and *chanachur* in a tray. Malkhan introduced him as his son. I was surprised to note the difference in their ages. Malkhan was around 75 though he did not appear to be more than 60 or 65. He explained that his first wife and child had to pay the price for him being a *baghi*; they had been killed. After surrendering and serving his term in prison, about 15 years back he remarried. He had a son and a daughter from this marriage. In between conversations an eight or nine-year-old girl in blue and black school uniform rushed inside and jumped upon Malkhan's lap. She looked at me in surprise and then kissed

Malkhan on his cheeks. Malkhan reciprocated her gestures. He looked at me and said, 'This is my daughter, Rajnandini.' He then asked her to go inside to change and freshen up. Turning towards me he said, 'Please go ahead with whatever you wish to ask.' Our conversation resumed.

Author: How many murders have you committed during your life as a *baghi*?

Malkhan Singh: See, I have not committed too many murders. The police had registered several false cases against me. In those days such things were common. If someone brings a false charge, a case is registered in your name. But those people could not identify me in jail. And you know how many false cases come up these days. Let me get this straight, I have hurt those who have hurt me. If a person destroys the lives of my hundred family members and I kill five of his, does it matter? You spoil the lives of around 250 of my family and friends, they have to move from door to door to survive; in return, I destroy two families. Then what's the big deal?

A: Alright, according to you, it was a fight against injustice. So how many persons did you kill during that fight?

M: They had tried to kill me in false encounters, arrest me, punish me. But what was my crime? My crime was that I was fighting for the temple land. I had only one demand—the land that belonged to Ram-Janaki's temple should belong to the temple only. Look, I have not killed anyone unnecessarily. Once I had requested the media with folded hands to write only what I said and not put words in my mouth. Prove it to me that I have committed one unjustified murder. You keep on writing that we have committed so many murders, have looted so many people, but where were you all when we were laying down arms in front of Arjun Singh? The court that was set up at that time had recorded my crimes. Why did you not find out from there whether I had killed 10 people or a hundred? Then you could have written the facts. And today, someone writes 100 or 150, is this the right way! See, the gang had committed some crimes. But unlike Phoolan in Behemai, we never committed mass killings.

A: Since you mentioned Phoolan, let me ask you, was there ever any woman in your gang?

M: We have never had any woman in our gang. I never allowed women to be a part of my gang because it is wrong to keep female members. Crimes increase if there are women in your gang. There is no difference in the lives of an ascetic and a *baghi*. Both lead a life of sacrifice. If there were a hundred men in a gang and only one woman, do you think that the gang will function? Won't there be fights within the gang?

(Since he considered Kamla to be his sister, he did not want to consider her a *baghi*. Moreover, Kamla did not stay in the *beehed* all the time.)

A: It seems you have a lot of anger against women?

M: Not at all. In our days, women could wear jewellery and go out even at midnight. We did not allow any rapes or any kind of nuisances. I have never encountered any incident of rape. Due to the stern principles of the *baghis* of Chambal, no one ever dared to commit such crimes. And look around yourself today. The pain of rape is compensated by doling out financial aid. There is rape and harassment of women all around you. I have extreme respect for your Chief Minister, Mamata *didi*. She leads the life of an ascetic. I respect such great women leaders and will continue to do so. I have always respected women. We have never looted a woman and have never allowed anyone to do so. This was the principle of my gang.

A: How many people did you abduct?

M: I have never abducted anyone. At times situations became such that we were compelled to abduct some people. But those were chiefly for arms. We had no food, no land, no house. What could we have done? But tell me, today there are so many cases of kidnapping across the country. What is their compulsion behind these acts? They are not even any registered gangs. If someone throws you out of your own house, what will you do? We did just that. I shall tell you what we did. If there were any disputes, we used to settle them. Suppose there was some land dispute. We used to intervene and solve the matter. This saved both the parties from running to court and they paid us a lakh or two in cash. We ran the gang with that money. We have not built houses for ourselves, nor accumulated any property. At times we did kidnap one or two people. In those days getting around Rs 10,000 or Rs 20,000 was enough. Unlike today, people did not have much money to pay a high ransom. Had we abducted more people, we would have been living in cities like Delhi or Mumbai, and not in this narrow lane of Gwalior. Have you noticed the road to my house while coming? It is unpaved with bricks and mortars coming out of it, showing its skeleton. If someone can prove that I have committed all these crimes, I swear in the name of Ram-Janaki, I am willing to serve my term in prison even now. I have never snatched anything from anyone, neither have I demanded anything from the government. At that time Rajiv Gandhi had said, 'If Malkhan does not want any land for himself, why is he taking so much time to surrender?' Rajiv Ji had returned the land to the temple; I went through the papers and surrendered. I did not have any sense of guilt. There are times when you have crime in your heart and there are crimes committed for selfish gains. But we had been forced to commit crimes.

A: Last year there was a Save the Beehed conference in Jaipur in which *baghis* were invited. Did you attend that?

M: No, I did not attend that because it was not organised properly. Was it a programme on the environment that you have titled Save the Beehed? What kind of a language is that? The government must save the *beehed*, save the mines. The government is not doing its duty. Will the *baghis* go and guard the *beehed* now or take their goats out there to graze! Big leaders are levelling the *beehed* and building farmhouses, while we are being asked to save the *beehed*! Had they organised a meeting regarding the problems of the *baghis*, about the unfulfilled promises of rehabilitation, and asked us to join that movement, I would have surely attended. In Chambal, land should have been distributed as promised and secondly, we won't let anyone sell Chambal. Had organisers raised their voices against foreign powers annexing land in Chambal to open companies, and said we won't let our mother be sold to foreigners, that would have had impact.

A: You have wasted so many years of your life in the *beehed*. What did you gain?

M: (Excited) Nothing except complete ruination. Does a dacoit have a room that does not even have a plaster? (He pointed at his drawing-room) A dacoit should have a very big house on two to three acres of land. He won't have a two-roomed house like this. Now you can only decide who is a dacoit and who isn't. Under compulsion, you can call me a dacoit or whatever you wish to. You people have the power so you have pushed us into the *beehed*. No one has heard us, our land has been snatched away, our wives and daughters have been insulted. I have spoken against all these injustices and if you call me a dacoit for that, it does not matter to me. I did what I had to do, you may do as you please.

A: Whose gang rules today's Chambal?

M: There are no gangs. There are no registered gangs as per government records. Don't you see today anyone with an affiliation to a political party moves around in a four-wheeler! The dacoits are in cities today. They move in their cars to kidnap people, harass women—none of them are *baghis*. All are rascals. There is a difference between dacoit and *baghi*. *Baghis* have their ideals. They used to fight against injustice and think about people. I, too, have helped in so many marriages, helped people during their times of need. But those who are in Chambal now, they commit crimes for their own interest, to serve their own purposes. These rascals must never be forgiven. They should be openly shot to death.

A: Why did you all become *baghis*? Was revenge the only reason?

M: A person does not become a *baghi*, he is made into one. And if you are made into a *baghi* then of course you will become one. Firstly, the land is not distributed properly, there is no proper justice, the ones who are in the wrong are saved because of their power, and those who raise their voices against injustice are branded as criminals. They get framed in false cases.

A: What is the difference between the *baghis* of earlier times and contemporary dacoits?

M: Earlier *baghis* were men of principles. One should not boast about oneself but as far as principles were concerned, it is said that even Mahatma can fail, but a *baghi* will never.

A: What is the situation of Chambal now?

M: It is in a very bad state. The forest department is destroying Chambal. They have ruined the lives of farmers too. They put up their boards at places where there are no saal or teak trees. These are fertile lands. Here the forest department should not intervene. They should be at places where there are big trees such as sesame and teak. Half the *beehed* consists of cultivable land but that is now full of weeds. If most of the *beehed* is levelled and each farmer is given around 10-20 bighas of land, there won't be any crime and no one will die of hunger. Everyone can lead a proper life then. In Chambal, it is not the government but the forest department that rules. There are no forests here. The officials of forest department simply sit and earn money. The entire place is filled with local thorny shrubs like babul, Dakshin bumra, and others. The forest department has not planted a single tree. You had been to my village Bilao. Have you seen any big trees there? The entire place is a jungle of Dakshin bumra.

A: What kind of relationship do you have with the police now?

M: Look, there had been confrontations between us quite often and in different areas. But no one had ever been killed. They did not do anything wrong; they were serving the law. They had their compulsions and we had ours.

Between conversations, Rajnandini arrived. She playfully bickered with Malkhan for some time. In the meantime, Malkhan's son also came to me and asked me to take his photo. Then Rajnandini, too, came up with the same request. I asked her to come and sit by me and started talking to her. She was studying in the third standard of a well-known English medium school. She wanted to become a doctor and treat people in the village of Bilao. She had been to the village with her father and was aware of the lack of any health centre in the village. The villagers have to travel a long distance to find a doctor. She also wanted to start a school in Bilao. Perfect successor to her father—I thought to myself! Once her father had chosen the life of a *baghi* to protest against the illegal usurpation of the temple land and exploitation of villagers by the Khangar Thakurs, and now his daughter dreams of providing education and medical facilities to the villagers of Bilao. Blood indeed shows its colours. At first, Malkhan did not want Rajnandini to be photographed. He had never allowed any media to take or post photographs of his family. But the loving father had to bow down to his beloved daughter's demands. He could be the fearful Baghi Samrat

Dadda Malkhan Singh for villagers, or gang members, or for the police records, but to this sweet little girl, he was just an affectionate father. He could hold his head high in front of police atrocities, he could revolt against government injustices, but he was completely helpless in front of the wishes of this innocent child. He had to acquiesce. I clicked Rajnandini's photograph. Then Malkhan's princess asked me to take another picture of her hugging her father. That wish was fulfilled too. Rajnandini then took a photograph of Malkhan and me. I asked Malkhan to pose with his gun but he said he did not possess any arms. Rajnandini chipped in immediately that there was a pistol in their almirah but before she could complete the sentence Malkhan shooed her away. My wish remained unfulfilled. Once again, we resumed our conversation.

A: Apart from rehabilitation, what were the other conditions that you had placed before the government before surrendering?

M: Nothing much. We had asked for a few things such as terms regarding land ownership, our rehabilitation, providing us with arms and license for security reasons, etc. but nothing happened. Some of us received some land, some did not. There are at least 10 more people who still have not received any land. The Congress ministry in Madhya Pradesh has been replaced by the BJP now. Now they say that the surrendering had happened in the name of Arjun Singh. But it did not happen in Arjun Singh's name, it took place on behalf of the Madhya Pradesh government. Whichever party forms the government, it remains a government responsibility. Whoever forms the government, can fulfil the promises. But if a government does not want to do so, then it is a different matter. Then let things go on the way they are!

A: What kind of security did the government provide you

with?

M: Some of us received licence for firearms. Some did not. But that is a different story. A private license for a gun, like the one you can procure in big cities like Kolkata, is not the same as a government license. You can get that for .315, the personal bores that you get for collector's items, LSR, etc. I believe that you have to keep on living, whether you get benefits from the government or not. What else is there in life!

A: How much land did you receive during rehabilitation and what other facilities were provided to you?

M: I did not receive any land for that purpose. Did I not just tell you that around 10 people are yet to receive any land? Some have received but 10 from my gang are still left. We are trying but our efforts are not showing any result. You know how these leaders work! The temple land for which I had been fighting has around a hundred acres. Some of it has been taken over by the temple priest and the rest of it is being enjoyed by others. The land is not being looked after properly. The secretary of the trust that looks after the land is the collector of Bhind. I am a member too. He had got that trust registered in the name of Ram-Janaki. Had the land been registered under some person's name, that person would have sold it off. Property corrupts people. So, I had emphasised that the land must be registered in the name of Ram-Janaki *mata* and no one else. Once land is registered in the name of God, no one can sell it. People might draw advantages from that plot of land but the land will remain. No one can destroy it. That's what I had wanted.

A: How do you earn your living?

M: I have some land of my own. I also own a house in Guna district. Being a farmer, I till my land myself. In my village Bilao, I have my relatives too. All the villagers are Kshatriyas there. I earn a comfortable living. What's the point in earning too much? The landless ones cry but so do the owners of huge factories who own acres of land. If you have to cry, cry before God. Why do you have to cry before those political leaders!

A: You are probably the last *baghi* of Chambal to surrender. Has there been any *baghi* since then?

M: There is no one in Chambal now. A *baghi* stands against injustice. There is a huge difference between *baghis* and robbers. For example, today we have scams, rapes, crimes, theft, looting, etc. The people who commit these are robbers. But their names are never declared. Take a look at Uttar Pradesh, the ones who are contesting elections are people with 15 or 20 murder charges against them. Some even have rape charges. These people are robbers. It is one thing to have that much wealth which will enable you to provide education and run the family properly but I do not want so much affluence that I lose my happiness and peace. I am currently a member of Lok Dal. Choudhury Charan Singh is our leader. I am a member of its national executive committee.

A: At one point of time, you had campaigned for the Congress party too?

M: (Dodging this question) *Arre bhai*, our party does not have any such criminals. Not a single person has any charge against him. Charan Singh Ji's party is spotless in this matter. Look at the other parties and the amount of hullabaloo that is being created by those sister-fuckers. Our national president is Ajit Singh Ji. His son is Jayant Singh Ji. It does not matter how many seats our party wins, it is Lok Dal that will form the government.

A: A few days back, you had even campaigned for the BJP.

M: Try and understand this. I am an independent individual, not a bonded labourer of any political party. Irrespective of the party with which I may be associated, I cannot tolerate injustice. If the BJP is in the wrong, if they do not listen to the people, if they exploit the poor, then I cannot like them. I am such a person who does not tolerate injustice even from my brother. I have spent my whole life fighting against injustice. If a party preaches something and does something else, I consider it a grave crime and hate such behaviour.

A: Was that the reason behind your quitting the BJP? Were such things happening within the party?

M: No, leaving a party and joining another is common. Did not I tell you that I am an independent individual? I can campaign for anyone, anywhere because no party has given me a ticket to contest elections, neither have I ever contested elections on behalf of any party. What do you understand by betrayal? When you are a member of a party for a decade or more, the party gives you a ticket to contest elections, it gives you a ministerial berth, and then you leave that party—that is betrayal. But I have never done so. I have always remained an independent voter and have asked people to vote independently too. Those who have stayed with the party for more than 20 years and then leave it are traitors. I shall always support the right candidate if you are a good person and you are doing good work. Whether it be BJP or the Congress, I shall support the party that does good work.

A: You said that dacoits were now politicians in this country. Who are you talking about?

M: Take a look around the country, so many great people are delivering speeches, campaigning for their candidates. I say that Modiji is a good person. He was feeding a cow in Varanasi yesterday (this was a reference to the Uttar Pradesh election where Modi had gone on an election campaign). I wanted to congratulate him. Being the Prime Minister of our country, he deserves to be congratulated. He is doing a lot of good work. It is good to seek votes for the party. All around the world politicians ask for votes for their respective parties. Just yesterday he was feeding a cow. He could have done that earlier too. Then so many cows would not have been slaughtered in our country. Unfortunately, he talks about the whole country, about Pakistan, asks the people to build Ram Mandir but nothing about the killing of cows. Look at your Kolkata. Cows are openly slaughtered there. You are an educated person, you tell me if such a thing is right. I am not bothered with religion, neither do I hate any religion. But I hate any injustice in the name of religion. Many people from this area are living in Kolkata. When they come here, they tell us about these things. Our *behenji*, Mamata di should stop these. She is such an austere woman. I respect her a lot! I admire her work as well as the commotion she creates. Whenever she says anything against anyone, she does it from her heart. There is one thing that I like the most about her. Whenever she speaks against any party, whether it is Congress or BJP, she is extremely earnest about it. Such great a female politician should always be respected. It would be great if *behenji* can do one thing in particular. The spiritedness with which she speaks about political leaders, if she could use it to speak on behalf of cows too, that would have been wonderful. This soil is infested with crimes. The soil has lost its heart. You can see it for yourself—the language of our political leaders during election campaigns is an example. They call each other names like donkey, dog, horse or lion. This is the first time that I am hearing such language during election campaigns! I don't understand who is a donkey or who is a dog or a lion. If such educated people speak in such dirty language, what will simple people like us do! We were just *baghis* in Chambal, without much education. But I never give false reports and no abuses ever come out of my mouth. (By then of course he had used quite a few choicest expletives.)

A: The government has not kept its promise of rehabilitation. What are you doing about it?

M: It's alright. We are continuing with our demands from the government in a proper way. Worshipping of Ram-Janaki is also going on smoothly. I had met the collector too.

A: A few days back there was a talk about making a movie on your life. What happened to that?

M: The film is almost complete but they have not been able to release it yet. Don't know by when they will be able to do it. That is something that the producers know. I have told them the story of my life. More than two years have passed now. I have told the producers that if they don't release the movie soon, I shall take back my story and file a case against them. I can also give my story to another director. I am waiting for some more time. Let's see what happens.

I figured out that Malkhan was not going to divulge any information because he was trying to construct an image of clean Chambal. He was working for various political parties and he was not going to get into the bad books of any. But I understood this much that he was quite annoyed with the BJP. Firstly, he did not receive any special treatment within the party. Moreover, in spite of being such a famous *baghi*, he had to stand in a long queue during demonetisation to withdraw money. A photograph of Malkhan, rifle strapped to his shoulder, standing in a long queue in front of an ATM counter, had made it to the newspaper headlines at that time. Malkhan was acting in a few films, there was also the talk of a biopic on his life—BJP leaders had sneered at all these. Malkhan took my phone number. He said that he would be coming to the city to buy a gun and asked me if I would help him then to reach the address at Ichhapur. Our conversation was almost over so I decided to take my leave. Malkhan walked me to the door.

It was just four in the evening, I still had time. I asked the auto driver to take me to Gwalior fort. Standing in front of that huge fort, I could feel my insignificance. Crossing the ups and downs I reached the top of the *beehed* to enter the fort. I have been to many forts across the country. But nothing can match the beauty of Gwalior fort in the soft light of the setting sun. There were cycles available on rent to see the entire fort—so big was its complex. It had a very rich museum too. There were antiquities spread across the fort. Those did not just belong to the times of Mansingh, but went much beyond. There were artefacts from the Gupta period and from even more ancient times. But this is not the time or place for the story of Gwalior fort, it will be for some other time. While walking around in Gwalior Fort, an idea suddenly struck me and I returned immediately.

During my trip to Chambal, I have seen that people from distant villages come to these hotels in search of livelihood. Most of them are landless villagers. I had seen such a person in the hotel where I was staying too. I thought of talking to him in the hope of getting some lead. I went straight to my room, ordered tea, and also called for that particular person. His name was Guchchha Singh. Tea arrived and I offered a seat to Guchchha. Giving him a hundred rupee note I said that I needed him to do something for me. He misunderstood my intention and asked, 'What kind of girl would you like?' I assured him that I did not want a girl but something else. He was confused. I explained to him my intention. I told him that I had come from Kolkata to know about the lives of *baghis*, and asked if he could put me in touch with some *baghis* or give me an address. He shook his head vehemently, got up, and left the room. Around eight in the evening, there was a knock on my door. Guchcha had brought my dinner. He looked around the room and said, '*Sahab* I do not know any dacoits but I can get you in touch with a person from my village. His name is Mohar Singh. In 2011 dacoit Pappu

Gujjar had cut off his hands and nose and parcelled it to the SP of Madhya Pradesh police as a gift.' 'When may I talk to him?' I asked. 'Tomorrow morning', Guchcha replied. But I was supposed to check out the next morning. Guchcha assured me that I would be able to talk to Mohar before leaving.

I had nothing more to do that day. The next day I was supposed to travel to Itawa. This region of Uttar Pradesh was a part of Chambal too and dacoits were a major problem here as well. Seema Parihar, Neelam Gupta, Kusuma Nain, and many such fearful women dacoits have been born in Itawa. Seema and Neelam were from the Auria district. My next stop was for one of them. I was not sure about being able to meet Seema because she was busy contesting elections. She was also participating in the Bollywood reality show—the Big Boss. So, it would be difficult to meet her. But I had come to know from various newspapers that in January 2017, Neelam Gupta had completed her 13 years of imprisonment and had returned home. So, she was my first target.

Bundelkhandi is perhaps the only language in Uttar Pradesh, Madhya Pradesh, and Rajasthan that an outsider would find harsh and impolite in tone. The *beehed* area which extends along the borders of Uttar Pradesh, Madhya Pradesh, and Rajasthan is not as uninhabited as it appears to be when one travels through trains or buses. The extremely complex topography of this region makes the villages difficult to access. One such village is Murawan in Sheopur district. To reach this place from Sheopur city, one has to cross a 12 kilometre stretch of thorny bushes. A person unaware of the proper path may reach their destination with cuts and bruises incurred along the way. That village is exactly like the Chambal that we have read about in stories. In October 2011, Pappu Gujjar entered the village and severed the arms and nose of a person called Mohar Singh to send those as a gift to the Superintendent of Police. He did that to spread his terror in the area. Even now if someone enters the village and asks for Mohar Singh, villagers express their disapproval in Bundelkhandi. They complain that 'The dacoits have made life hell for us. Ever since Pappu Gujjar had chopped off Mohar Singh's hands and nose, we are living in constant fear. He has threatened us that if a *chabutara* is not built at Murawan in the name of his ring leader, Rajendra Gatta, and if his other demands are not fulfilled, he will kill all the people of this village and Hatheri village.'

In 2011, Pappu Gujjar was the latest name in the list of dacoits in Chambal. He was the brother of another infamous dacoit, Rajendra Gatta. Gatta was active in 2009-10 in the areas around Sheopur, Shivpuri, and Ashoknagar in Madhya Pradesh as well as in Dhaulpur, Banra, and Sawai Madhopur in Rajasthan. There was a prize on his head. Gatta, against whom there were cases of a dozen murders, kidnapping, and robberies, was killed by the members of his gang. This took place in January 2011 and the police discovered his body from a temple near Murawan village. Since then, Pappu, Gatta's brother was the leader of this gang. According to the police, this gang had kidnapped an important businessman from Rajasthan and extorted a sum of 20 lakh from him. There was a quarrel within the group regarding the distribution of that money. And according to Pappu Gujjar, his brother had around three lakh rupees in cash, five grams of gold, and 159 bullets on him which had been stolen later by the villagers. That was the reason why Pappu had chopped off Mohar's hands and nose and gifted them to the Superintendent of Police of Sheopur district, Mahendra Singh Shekarwar. He had also sent a letter along with the parcel that if the lost bullets, gold, and money were not retrieved immediately, he would kill all the villagers of Hatheri and Murawan. Hatheri was an adivasi village, about eight kilometres from Murawan which the dacoits often attacked to demand food. Apart from the *chabutara,* Pappu has also asked the villagers of Murawan to organise a feast on the death anniversary of Rajendra Gattar.

Due to such threats, the villagers of Hatheri have left their homes, harvest, and village and ran away.

What did the police do to deal with such threats? An official unwilling to reveal his name said, 'We increased the security of the entire area and even deployed some policemen in Morawan and Hatheri. After Gatta's death, there were two gangs active in this area—one led by Pappu Gurjar and the other by Kalli Gurjar. Our anti-dacoit team came up with a plan to execute these two gangs.' But despite the assurances from police, the people of these two villages lived in fear. Hatheri was a small village on the Kuno river bank, inside the Palpur-Kuno forest, approximately 18 kilometres away from the Sheopur main road. It was inhabited by about 40 tribal families. One of the villagers of Hatheri, Guchcha Singh, spoke to me, 'We were facing a huge problem regarding the dacoits. They used to demand flour, rice, and other food items from us whenever they felt like. We could somehow manage two square meals ourselves. From where could we provide for them! If we did not give them the ration, they attempted to kill us and if we did, the police arrested us. We were suffering from both ends. That year we had to leave our crops unharvested and flee from the village.' Guchcha Singh said, on that fateful evening Pappu entered the village along with his companions and chopped off Mohar's arms and nose in front of everyone. He also asked for money but we had nothing to give. So, we somehow managed to run away from that place with our lives. It was only in 2017 that around eight or ten families dared to return to the village.

Most Chambal enthusiasts keep themselves confined to stories of Mansingh, Malkhan Singh, or Phoolan Devi. But according to experts, dacoity has been a part of Chambal for quite a few centuries. Local author, Manmohan Kumar Tamanna, who has written several popular novels and stories on dacoits says that the *beehed* has been the ideal place for guerrilla warfare for more than a century. As mentioned earlier, the famous Chinese traveller during Harshavardhana's period, Huen Tsang, was looted by the dacoits at a place located near modern-day Dhaulpur. Prithviraj Chauhan too spent his life as a *baghi* in Chambal after his defeat in Delhi. There is a tale from the Mughal period, quite popular in Chambal. It is said that once when Akbar was travelling through this area, about 40 horses of his army were stolen. A party of soldiers went in search, but failed, and as a result, earned the death penalty from the king. Even today, local people proudly say that Akbar and his men could not find the horses because they were stolen by Gurjars. In the history of Chambal, the 1960 incident of a large number of dacoits surrendering themselves in front of Vinoba Bhave is considered to be the first such incident. But that is not the case. In 1920, Madhavrao Scindia (the great grandfather of Jyotiraditya Scindia, the king of Gwalior and Member of Parliament) had made 97 dacoits surrender. That was the first case of mass surrendering in Chambal.

It was quite early in the morning when someone knocked on my door. I was not even fully awake when I opened the door to see Guchcha Singh. He rushed into my room and shut the door immediately. I was a bit surprised by his actions. He began, 'The dacoits have made it difficult for us to live. From the day Pappu Gujjar had cut off Mohar's hands and nose, everyone is living in great fear. He has threatened the villagers that if they do not build a *chabutara* in the name of his ring leader, Rajendra Patta, and fulfil his other demands, he would kill everyone living in Hatheri and this village. Both these villages are situated on the bank of Kuno river in the Palampur-Kuno forest which is 18 kilometres from the highway. All the villagers here belong to Saheria and Mantha tribes. Quickly talk to him from my phone otherwise even he will not talk later.' Saying this, he pushed the phone into my palms. I spoke to Mohar.

Author: Mohar, don't be scared. No one will come to know of you.

Mohar Singh: We are scared *sahib*. I am completely ruined. Now I only have my life.

A: Why did Pappu cut your hands?

M: Before Pappu, his brother Rajendra Gatta was the leader of this gang. In January 2011 his corpse was discovered by the police from a temple in our village. The police said that the dacoits had received about 20 lakh rupees as ransom by kidnapping a rich businessman from Rajasthan and Gatta was killed in the encounter with the police during the distribution of that money among the gang members. But the whole village knows what the actual truth is. Gatta was killed by his men over a dispute regarding the distribution of that money. Now Pappu says that when his brother died, he had about three lakh rupees, 50 grams of gold, and 156 cartridges with him which the villagers have stolen. Hence, to teach the entire village a lesson, he cut off my hands and nose.

A: Did the villagers steal the money?

M: What are you saying *sahib*! The villagers have very small plots of land which they cultivate and somehow earn a living. They cannot even earn two meals a day. Where will they keep so much wealth! And even if someone steals it, where will he spend it? He would be caught immediately. And how will he even sell the gold? No one will buy it. And the cartridges—what shall we do with those? None of us own a gun.

A: But then why did Pappu chop off your hands and nose? And where did the money and other things vanish?

M: *Sahib*, all these are games played by the police. Had they not spread the news of that fake encounter, none of this would have happened. The police must have removed the money and gold. They were the ones near the body.

A: Do you remember what exactly happened on that day?

M: How can I not remember? I can never forget that day. It was an evening in October. I had just returned from the fields and was smoking a bidi sitting at my doorstep. My wife was busy cooking. Suddenly, around 8 or 9 pm I saw a group of seven or eight men with guns strapped to their shoulders coming towards my house. I got scared. They came and kicked me out in the courtyard. One kept a gun pointed towards me and the rest asked my wife to cook for them. Once the food was prepared, they sat upon the charpoy and ate. I thought that they would leave after that. But out of the blue one of them slapped me hard, twice and said, 'The police and villagers have accumulated a lot of fat. You people must have informed the police about my brother. And you all must have stolen the gold and money.' Thereafter, they tied me to the charpoy. I kept saying that I did not know anything, but they were unwilling to listen. Someone hit upon my hand with something. I don't remember anything after that. When I opened my eyes, it was morning and I was in the hospital. Both my hands were missing and my face was swollen. Then I came to know that they had cut off my arms and nose.

A: Did the police not do anything?

M: What will the police do *sahib*? They came to the hospital, took my statement, and went away. Some newspaper reporters had come but I did not tell them anything. I had already lost my hands and nose. I did not want to lose my life too! I have my family to think of. Before they left even my wife was… (I could hear him crying on the other side of the phone and the call was disconnected after that.)

After five more minutes, we could once again connect with Mohar on phone. Before calling up Guchcha Singh warned me, 'His wound is still fresh, question him carefully.'

A: Did the government not do anything for you?

M: Oh yes! I got free treatment; my wife got 5,000 rupees. What else! Even God does not give anything to the poor, how much can these leaders do!

A: How do you run your family?

M: I have five bighas of land. My wife and son grow crops on it. We somehow manage to survive on that.

A: Don't you get any help from the villagers?

M: How will they help me? They do not have enough to eat. All of us in this village and the next belong to the Saheriya tribe. Scared of Pappu's threats, they left their land and crops and ran away. There used to be 40 families in the village. Now there are only 10. All others have escaped to Morena. I have been marred by fate. It is a sin to be poor in this world. When you have taken birth in a poor family, you will have to suffer.

I could not talk anymore and disconnected the phone. I could not question Mohar as a journalist anymore. Later I heard from an employee at the hotel that those dacoits had gang-raped his wife that night. Mohar is scared of the tradition of revenge that has become an integral part of the history of Chambal and hopes that it leaves his son unharmed. I shall not be surprised if someday I come to know that Mohar's son has taken up arms after losing faith in the law and order of the country. And why shouldn't he! What was his parents' fault? Gatta was killed by his men but police wanted to take credit for it. Also, it was the police who had removed the money, gold, and cartridges from Gatta. But it is the common people who are bearing the brunt of it. To add insult to injury, the government had absolved itself of its responsibility by providing free treatment to Mohar and giving only 5,000 rupees to his wife. When the only earning member of the family loses his hands and nose, he also loses his capability to earn. How long can a family survive on 5,000 rupees? Neither the government nor any leader has given any thought to it. Hence, if

Mohar's son takes up arms in the future, he cannot be blamed for it. The history of Chambal has numerous examples of false encounters by the police. Time and again police have taken credit for dacoits killed due to internal rivalry. In many cases, when women had come to the police to report abuses and tortures, the police had refused to take complaints. Instead, they took bribes from abusers, who are generally influential men in villages. And, the police called these women to the police station at night and repeatedly abused them physically. The police often rape rape-survivors. We have such examples in Putli Bai, Phoolan Devi, and Kusuma Nain. More than dacoits, it is the police who have disgraced Chambal. I remembered Malkhan's words, '*Baghis* are not born, they are created.' This is the ultimate reality of Chambal. Even the government is responsible. They have not fulfilled even one-fourth of their promises made to the *baghis* during their surrender. Therefore, finding all doors closed, these exploited human beings have once again picked up their guns.

I checked out of the hotel to start for my next destination—Itawa in Uttar Pradesh. From there I would go to Auria prison. I took an Uttar Pradesh state bus from Gwalior. Itawa was at a distance of 117 kms, a journey of three and a half hours. As the bus moved ahead, I kept looking at River Chambal, the forest far away, and the *beehed*. Hidden between them were so many painful tales. I could not collect most of them due to lack of time. 12 days of travelling in Chambal were too short for the purpose. To know this place properly, one must stay here for months and interact with the place at a much deeper level. Only then the truth might be revealed. *Abhisopto Chambal, Baghi, Behed, Bandook,* or this book—all reveal partial truths about Chambal. Deeper truths can be found in the forests of Chambal and *beehed*. It would take a whole lifetime to dig all of them out.

After reaching Itawa, I checked into a hotel near the bus terminus. Dusk had set in so it was not possible to go out anywhere. I wandered along the nearby area and then retired to my room. The next morning, I would go to Auria to look for Neelam Gupta. She was one of the contemporary women dacoits of Chambal. Chambal has seen some extraordinary female dacoits. The first was Putli Bai, then there were Phoolan Devi, Kusuma Nain, Seema Parihar, and many more. The lives of these women were no less adventurous. Chambal Valley has been the witness to their love stories, their experiences of motherhood as well as their fight against injustice. But many of these women, who were once the terror of Chambal, are fighting a different battle today to provide a better life to their children. When a woman escapes into the *beehed* with a gun, she attracts more attention. In Chambal, there have been hundreds of women whose names spelt terror. Some of them are active even now. The wife of Chhaviram, an infamous dacoit of Chambal, had gone through a lot of struggles to get a respectable life for her child. She educated him and today he is a police inspector in Uttar Pradesh. Seema Parihar's child was born in the *beehed*. There was a time when Seema and terror were synonymous. Before her life in the *beehed*, Seema lived an ordinary life with her parents. Dacoit leader Lalaram kidnapped her and brought her to the *beehed*. Later he got her married to Nirbhay, a member of his gang. Nirbhay and Seema's child was born in the *beehed*. But very soon the couple separated because Nirbhay was a womaniser. He had a relationship with Lalaram's wife Kusuma too. Seema wants to provide a healthy and normal life to her child. Currently on bail, Seema Parihar is actively involved in politics and works from the Auria district. She will also contest the election from Phoolan Devi's constituency, Mirzapur. Apart from Seema, Renu Yadav, wife of dacoit Chandan Yadav, had also given birth to her daughter in the *beehed*. Presently their daughter is living with her grandmother in Mangalpuri, Auria. Komse Gurjar, a woman dacoit belonging to the gang of the notorious Jagat Gurjar also became a mother while in the *beehed*, despite all the dangers that accompanied a life there. She had taken up arms and chose to live in the *beehed* to avenge the death of her father, Chitiriya Gurjar, a retired *sarpanch* in a village in Dhaulpur district in Rajasthan. As a member of Jagat or Jagan's gang, Komse became quite close to him. During a confrontation with the Madhya Pradesh police in Murena, Komse was wounded by a bullet. Jagat somehow managed to escape with her. But on 5 November 2008, Komse was arrested from a nursing home in Samarpura, Dhaulpur where she was undergoing treatment. Jagat could not bear this separation from Komse and he became desperate to meet her. Finally on 31 January 2009, at the Jagdish Temple Complex in Kemri village of Kareli district in Rajasthan, he laid down his arms in front of Congress MP Rajesh Pilot on the condition that he would be kept in the same jail as Komse. After surrendering, an emotional Jagat had stated that he wanted to live the rest of his life like a common person. In the eighties, after Seema Parihar, many other women such as Lovely Pandey, Arati, Anita Dikshit, Neelam Gupta, Sarala Jatav, Sapna Soni, Renu Yadav, Sunita Pandey, Gangasree had chosen a life in the *beehed*. Though once Lovely Pandey was more notorious than other women dacoits, no one could gain as much popularity as Seema Parihar. Among these women, except for Sarala Jatav, Neelam Gupta, and Renu Yadav, others lost their lives to police encounters. We all know the story of Phoolan Devi so I would not be narrating her story here. The narrative on women dacoits of Chambal should begin with the story of Putli Bai, the first woman dacoit of this area—Putli Bai whose house I had seen with my own eyes at Barabai village in Amba tehsil.

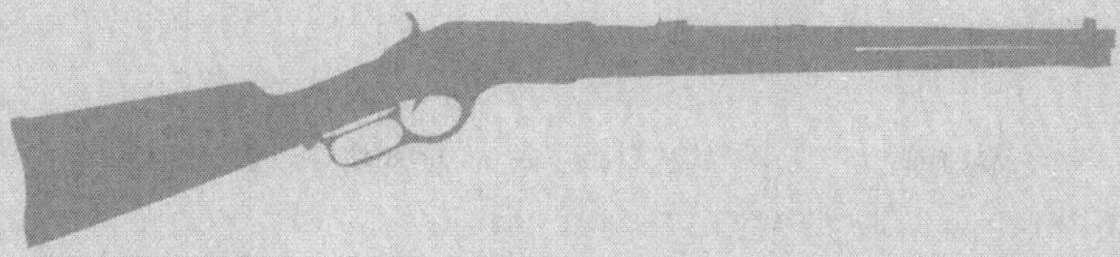

DACOIT BEAUTY PUTLI BAI

Chambal has not only experienced the terror of Mansingh, Mohar Singh, Malkhan Singh, or Rupa Maharaj, but it has also experienced the dread of Putli Bai, Phoolan Devi, Kusuma Nain, Seema Parihar, and Neelam Gupta. Chambal had long been the dominion of imposing moustaches and masculine prowess. For any common person, just to move about in Chambal, to sleep and wake up in the bolt holes of the *beehed* was nothing less than punishment. To become a *baghi* meant making this difficult place home. In Chambal, it was not just guns but even mouths that shot out bullets as a mark of their masculinity. Until the fifties, no one could imagine a woman taking up arms in the *beehed*, leave alone becoming one of the most formidable dacoits! But Chambal's stories are full of twists and turns like its eponymous river. So there came such a character in Chambal whose story would put even a Hollywood movie to shame. Even Calcutta was not spared from her dread. She was Putli Bai—the first woman dacoit in the *beehed* of Chambal. But the story of a woman becoming the queen of Chambal is both fascinating and tragic, to say the least. At each turn, the story seems to come to an end, but it does not. Instead, it moves forward. The woman who stole millions of hearts with her performances could also send shivers down the spine with a gun in her hand. She was equally adept at shooting with both her hands and when one of her arms was wounded by a police bullet, she did not hesitate to cut it off. But the loss of her hand could not dent her confidence, in certain ways, she became even more formidable. She used to rain bullets upon the police using just one hand. Before coming to the *beehed*, Putli was famous for her attractive figure, melodious voice, and captivating dances. The journey of her life that began as a performing artist ended with her attaining the position of the bandit queen who could twirl entire Chambal on her little finger. She had nothing to do with the *baghis* of Chambal. Though she used to perform for dacoits too, their interaction was limited to the duration of the performance. It was Putli Bai's popularity as a dancer that forged her relationship with the *beehed*. It was a bond of love and when that broke, it became a source of great sorrow that ultimately culminated in bonding with the gun. And the gun remained with her until her death. For Putli Bai, Chambal provided her with a livelihood as well as her final resting place. That Putli who could mesmerise Chambal with magical melodies was lost in the noise of gunshots. Putli's story today has become an inseparable part of Chambal's tales. But who was this Putli Bai? What was her origin?

Barbai is a small village in the Ambah *tehsil* of Murena district. The first thing that one comes across on entering this village is Pandit Ram Prasad Bismil Park. Ram Prasad Bismil had a deep connection with this village. This great freedom fighter who had written patriotic songs like *Sarfaroshi ki tamanna*, and on the day of his execution, embraced the noose singing this song, belonged to this place. He was the leader associated with the Kakori conspiracy case. On 9 August 1925, a group of revolutionaries had looted government money from a running train to support their revolutionary activities. Ram Prasad was awarded death sentence following the trial on this case.

At a little distance from Ram Prasad Bismil Park, one could see the remains of a house with dilapidated walls, termite-infested joists, without any doors or windows. The crumbling walls narrated a 70-year old story. That house is now divided into various sections, separately bought by some villagers. The part that remains unsold speaks of a long wait for the sounds of *ghungroo* or beats on the *tabla*, as if it is waiting to go back to its youth through the songs of Asgari Bai and the dances of Putli Bai. Putli's brother and his family have sold off as much of the house as they could and left the village. Only some portions from Putli's part are left unsold. On one of its walls is a small nook to keep an earthen lamp—once upon a time, Putli used to perform in its light. That lamp has not been lit since her death. There is nothing to see when one peeps in through the weed entangled window because there is nothing left in that room. That room, the place from where Putli's journey began, has remained locked ever since her daughter Tanveer Banno left the village. Putli was born to Asgari Bai, belonging to the *berni* community of performers. The lifestyle of the *bernis* is similar to that of the *banjaras*.

Asgari Bai was extremely beautiful and it was said that Putli Bai had inherited her beauty from her mother. Both Putli Bai and her sister, Tara Bai, received lessons in music and dance from an early stage. They began their career as performers from this house. After a few days, Asgari realised that the village was too small a place for Putli Bai. So, she took her to Agra, the city that knew the value of talent. Putli started performing in a small room in the city. Her melodious voice and electrifying dances soon became popular throughout the city. Very soon Asgari Bai's *kotha* became the best one in the city. With Putli's rising popularity, they started earning more. Putli's rich voice by then had reached other cities such as Lucknow, Kanpur, etc. Wherever she performed, money rained on them. Meanwhile, along with the forms she was familiar with, Putli mastered two more forms—the *alha* and *Holi* songs. *Alha* was a part of life in Chambal and Bundelkhand which sang about the brave deeds of Alha and Udal. Putli Bai sang them with such dedication that even expert singers of the area would bow down to her performance. With affluence, their lifestyle began changing too. Police, too, became aware of her popularity. Many police officers started frequenting her *kotha* and they took so much interest in her that other clients maintained a distance from her. Putli Bai was gradually turning into a private performer for a few officials. Agsari Bai was worried by the turn of events and she immediately left Agra with Putli to return to her village and city, Barbai and Murena. She started anew in Murena and also visited nearby places. During one such journey, suddenly Putli's life changed forever and her life in Chambal began.

Putli was asked to perform at the wedding of the son of a rich zamindar of Dhaulpur in Rajasthan. She knew she would be handsomely paid for such a performance and hence started for Dhaulpur with her mother and brother. She mesmerised everyone with her performance. Money and alcohol flowed freely. Around 2 am when the performance was at its peak, suddenly sounds of firing brought a deathly silence. Immediately lights were put off. *Tabla* and *sarangi,* too, stopped playing. Sitting upon an expensive carpet, Putli Bai was just about to take off her *ghunghroo* when suddenly two strong hands pulled her up. Before anyone could understand, Putli was abducted and taken to the *beehed* on horseback. There is another version of this story. When Putli was returning from her performance with her troupe one night, the dreaded dacoit, Sultana, and his people obstructed their way. But like other *baghis,* Sultana too had never insulted any woman. Putli was not at all scared and asked to know who he was. In a deep voice, he replied, 'Your admirer—Sultana.' Putli tried to avoid him but Sultana was completely smitten by her beauty and youth. To prevent her from escaping, he pointed his gun at her brother. Putli gave herself up to Sultana to save her brother's life. Sultana took her to his den in the *beehed*. That very night they had set up a stage where Putli's spectacular dance was accompanied by unlimited liquor.

In Chambal, rumours spread faster than wind. And this time, the gossip contained both a woman and liquor. In no time, every village in Chambal came to know that Putli Bai had joined Sultana to become a *baghi*. Sultana started bringing expensive gifts for Putli. That needed money. So, Sultana increased his frequency of robberies. Putli was scared to see so much violence, killing, and loot. She begged Sultana to let her go. At first, Sultana did not agree, but Putli started getting nightmares and kept shouting in her sleep. Sultana tried to talk her out of it but by then Putli was determined to return. Sultana explained to her that a *baghi* did not have any home to return to. One could return from any other place but once someone takes this road, there was no point of return. Putli started starving herself. Finally, Sultana had to relent. He let her return. He accompanied her to a nearby village in the *beehed* and said while leaving, 'The world will not accept you anymore Putli.' Though Putli wanted to return home, fate had something else in store for her.

The news of her returning home spread immediately. Before she could even rest for a while, the police arrived. She had to go to the police station with them. It is said that she was tortured for hours by the police and was administered various degrees of pain but she did not divulge any information regarding Sultana and his gang. The police continued torturing her for several days. She was called to the police station even at night. Seventy years ago, there were only two kinds of law in Chambal—in the forest, it was the dacoits and, in the cities, the police. Neither the dacoits had any law that could bind them, nor was there any limits to the unlawful practices of the police. It became a routine for them to summon Putli to the police station or to take her to officers' bungalows and make her do their bidding. At such a stage, Putli remembered her days in the *beehed* where Sultana's gang respected her as their leader's wife. Though Babu Lohar, the second-in-command in Sultana's gang had eyes on her, he could not do anything because of Sultana. Meanwhile, Putli Bai gave birth to a daughter. She was pregnant while she was in the *beehed* and did not want her child to be born in that vicious environment. Lovingly, she named her daughter, Tanveer Banno or Tanno for short. Two months after the birth of her daughter, Putli started performing once again. Then one day, during a performance at a place near Barbai, she sent for Sultana. This time she accompanied him to the *beehed*. Putli was tired of the atrocities of the police and society, and this time she chose to return to the *beehed* on her own accord. But there was a change in her and she was no more scared of robberies or killing people.

Amid a lot of enthusiasm, the gang celebrated the return of Putli Bai. Slowly, she started helping out with their work. Initially, she was given the responsibility of distributing the loot after every robbery. But Sultana wanted to make her a complete *baghi*, one who would be an expert in handling all kinds of weapons. He gradually started training her. Within a few days, Putli mastered the skill of shooting with all kinds of guns. One day Sultana handed her a gun and asked her to shoot a member of the gang. Her initial hesitation was wiped away by Sultana's scolding and she shot that man right in between his forehead. That incident created history in Chambal. She attained the distinction of being the first woman *baghi* in Chambal by killing a police inspector. In the first case against her, the police record reads, 'Songs of brave deeds of Alha had such an impact on Putli Bai's mind that she started interpreting those acts of heroism in her own way. Thereafter, breaking the law became a new kind of game for her. Putli Bai, who once used to sing and dance, now became a dacoit in Sultana's gang for whom the law was nothing more than some rules to break.' Putli immersed herself in the game of robbery and killings. She became an active member of Sultana's gang.

The one thing that she could not forget was her daughter whom she had left behind. She was restless to see her. She told Sultana that she wanted to visit her daughter for a day and then return to him. Initially, Sultana did not agree. But later, Sultana agreed to the plan that when the gang would leave for robbery, she was to quickly slip out to see her daughter and then return quietly. But when the gang was just about to step out of the *beehed*, firing started. A big battalion of police surrounded the gang. Sultana shouted to her—'The police! hide yourself Putli!' Amid heavy firing, Sultana managed to escape with his gang. Putli remained hiding in the *beehed* but when she stepped out after some time, she found the police waiting there. She surrendered herself. She thought that the police would not frame her. She thought that they would let her go after keeping her in jail for some time, and that, then she could go back to her daughter.

The police first took her to Tajgunj in Agra and from there to Dhoulpur jail. She was released on bail from there. But Putli had become a puppet in the hands of the police by then. They did not agree to let her go to Murena and offered her two conditions. One, if she had to go to Murena, her sister Tara Bai must stay back in Dhaulpur. Or, Putli would have to become a spy for the police in Sultana's gang. But Putli did not agree to either of these. So, the police officers started frequenting her place with new and unreasonable demands each day. Finally, one day Putli relented. Relieved, the police officers removed the watch from her house and promised a liquor party for the evening. But when one of the police officers along with two of his men reached there in the evening, they found an empty nest. Putli managed to escape to the *beehed*. But this time when she went to Sultana, he asked her to go back to the city. Babu Lohar had poisoned Sultana's ears against Putli Bai, alleging her of acting as a spy for the police.

Babu made Sultana believe that the confrontation in Rajoi village had happened because Putli had informed the police. But hungry and thirsty, Putli did not leave the gang. After staying without water and food for almost four days, Sultana softened his attitude. He agreed to take her back in the gang. This time Putli had come intending to take revenge. As soon as she joined the gang she started with her actions. She targeted all those police officers and their families who had harassed her. Whenever she carried out her operations, she killed anyone who crossed her path and cut off one of their fingers. She also used to tear off women's ears along with their earrings. In Chambal, Putli Bai became another name for cruelty.

During this period, to grow his gang in size, Sultana invited Lakshman Singh to join him. At that time Lakshman Singh was considered the most ferocious dacoit in Chambal. When Putli met Lakshman for the first time she felt he might become a threat to the gang. Fate, too, must have silently laughed at that time. No member of either gang could tolerate each other, but Sultana placed his trust in Lakshman. To trust another person was against Chambal's law. It was believed that the one who trusted did not receive a proper burial. On 25 May 1955 the two gangs met at Arjunpur village under Murena police station to resolve their differences. The meeting had just started when the police surrounded them with all kinds of modern weaponry like brain guns, sten guns, etc. Very soon the gang crumbled before them like straw in the wind. Sultana's most trusted companion, Matadin, died. Then Sultana asked Babu Lohar to take Putli Bai to a safe shelter. Putli hid behind a hillock and kept watching. It was then that she saw Lakshman Singh signal towards Kalla dacoit. The latter pointed his rifle at Sultana, who was busy firing at the police, and was shot dead. Putli's entire world crumbled, as she was once again caught in the darkness of uncertainty. After the encounter, police found Sultana's body among other dead bodies. They took credit for killing him.

But according to the story of Chambal, Putli had later written a letter to the then prime minister, Jawaharlal Nehru, stating that Sultana had died in the hands of his gang members. The police refused to accept that.

With the death of Sultana, Putli's life became a kite without a string—anyone could take advantage of her. Even before the last rites of Sultana were over, Babu Lohar assumed the role of the leader of the gang. That very night he declared that he would rape Putli to avenge his insult. That night, along with Babu, Pahara Singh also raped her. Helpless Putli remained silent. She had no option but to wait for an opportunity. And, very soon she got a chance as well. About four months later, the gang faced police firing again, at a place called Khan-ki-Bhuinya, in another part of Murena. When bullets rained from all sides, the dacoits tried to save themselves by escaping to the road that led to Miragpur. Putli told Babu, 'Watch that mound over there and find out if the police are coming from that side.' The moment Babu turned that way, her rifle fired at him. Her revenge was complete but, once again, police took credit for killing Babu Lohar. Once again, Putli wrote a letter to the Prime Minister. The dispute regarding the actual killer of Babu Lohar was reported in newspapers as well. After this incident, Pahara Singh reached an understanding with Putli Bai and they started staying together. They also had a son together who was named Surendra. But Putli Bai could not stay even with Pahara for long. One day Pahara, too, lost his life to police bullets. Thereafter, Kalla accepted Putli as his leader. She became the chief of the gang with Kalla being second-in-command. He said that if Putli Bai wanted, she could go back to her former life of music and dance. But by then Putli knew that stepping out of the *beehed* would mean an end to her life. Amid all these confusions, it is said that she, once again, wrote a letter to Prime Minister Nehru in 1956. In that letter, she narrated her entire story and asked whether the law would grant her pardon if she wanted to return to a normal life. But she did not receive any response from him. Putli now turned into the bandit queen, Putli Bai.

Their gang became known as the Kalla-Putli gang and their notoriety sent shivers across Chambal. But fate had other plans for Putli. One day, during a confrontation with the police at Gormi in Bhind, the police saw Putli firing straight at them, while holding her infant son in another hand. During the firing, one police bullet entered into Putli's shoulder. Kalla picked her up and escaped from there.

For the next two months, police kept following the trail of her blood to find her but failed to do so. Then one day, the police was informed that the entire gang had taken shelter in Khitauli village. Four platoons of police surrounded the village and started searching for the dacoits. When the police had just finished searching in two of the houses and were moving towards the third, suddenly heavy firing began. One bullet pierced the breast of a high official. Before his death, the officer stated that he had been shot by Putli Bai and that she had just one hand. The right-handed Putli Bai had cut off her left hand. The entire gang escaped from that village. But nobody could believe that a woman with one arm could shoot a police officer. After a few days, there was another confrontation at Kanaripura. There was an attack from the police when the gang was settling down for lunch. But they managed to escape even then. They found Putli Bai's lipstick from the site and a few police officers saw one-armed Putli running away. After investigations, the police came to know that Putli had paid 20,000 rupees to a doctor and made him amputate her left hand from the elbow.

Losing her hand seemed to have wiped away any signs of femininity from her personality. She also lost all sense of pain and became completely addicted to bloodshed and violence. Chambal was left strewn with corpses of her victims. According to one police report, in December 1957 only the

Kalla-Putli gang had looted 75,000 rupees and killed six people in just two robberies. Bhind, Murena, Shivpuri, and Gwalior lived in constant terror of this gang. On the other hand, Lakshman's gang too continued with robberies and bloodshed. The government was forced into action and it decided to tackle Lakshman first, then Putli. But time always has its own story. Putli was just 27 then. Though she was quite young, it was also the stage where her life would come to a complete stop. On 23 January 1958, police received information that Lakshman had taken refuge in Konthar village in Murena. A huge police force was deployed outside the village. All the roads that Lakshman's gang could take to escape were blocked. To make the siege foolproof, they even deployed police in all the villages across Kunwari river. There were armed police present in Arusi, Sihonia, Lepa, Sangoli, Tarsama, and many other nearby villages. Then the wait began. I had heard the description of those days from a police officer unwilling to disclose his name.

Here is what he narrated to me, 'Each moment seemed longer than an age. After a long time, one of our troupes noticed a group of 10 to 15 people coming from Tarsama village. Immediately a section of our force was sent towards them. But sudden firing from their side surprised us because in more than a decade as a dacoit, Lakshman Singh and his gang had never engaged themselves in any face-to-face confrontation with the police. Then our leader Kailash Singh shouted excitedly—that is Putli's gang! Without wasting a moment Kailash-ji ordered us to surround the gang. Acting upon the order, we too communicated via walkie-talkie and asked our other groups to surround them as well. Kalla understood the gravity of the situation. He immediately divided the gang into two sections. He went in one direction with five dacoits and asked 10 other dacoits to accompany Putli towards the Kunwari river. There was just a field of black grams between Putli and the river, so she thought that if she could run across the field to reach the river then she could swim it and enter the *beehed*. Once in the *beehed*, she would be beyond police firing because without prior preparation no police force could carry on an assault there. But fate had other plans that day. All the dacoits who were accompanying Putli had lost their lives by then. She was all alone when she ran across the field. Even at that time, her presence of mind was commendable. In those days, the police did not draw a handsome salary. In the middle of such heavy firing, she started throwing away the currency notes that she was carrying in her pocket. All of a sudden, the constables started fighting amongst themselves for that money. She used that opportunity to jump into the river. The first thing she did was to take off her coat and pants and then with one hand, she swam to the other bank. But as soon as she raised her head, she knew that the stage had been set for her end that day. Our police force was present on the other side of the river too. The moment the police waiting on the other side saw Putli, they started firing and that was the end of Putli Bai's life.'

The police officer who told me this did not want his name published, as some information that he divulged to me could have landed him into trouble. After her death, the police played a dirty game with her corpse which had created quite an uproar in national politics. Tarun Bhaduri had mentioned those dark deeds of the police in his work *Beehed, Baghi, Bandook*, but even he was not quite sure about the authenticity of these reports. The police officer I spoke to was a part of that force that had killed Putli Bai that day. He was just a sepoy in the police at that time. The description that I heard from him would be enough to put any human being to shame. Though a criminal, Putli was a human being, a woman. She had died in the encounter. And it was beyond comprehension that a civilized society could disrespect the dead in such a manner! The same officer described in detail what had exactly happened after the encounter that day.

'We were in a celebratory mood. We had come to finish Lakshman Singh, but in his place, we encountered Putli. It was the greatest success that we had achieved till then. Though Lakshman was a dreaded *baghi*, his was nothing compared to Putli's atrocities. We dragged Putli's naked body and tied her behind a tractor. The corpse was dragged all along the way to the village. Though other corpses were kept in the tractor, Putli's body remained tied there and that was how she was taken to Murena. The crowd gathered from all over to see the bandit queen Putli Bai for one last time. Actually, we had wanted to set an example for *baghis*. We also reached the end of our patience with these dacoits. Day after day we had to carry on fighting them, often at the cost of our lives. To add to that was the pressure from our superiors. We were at the brink of tolerance. I don't know why, but that day we were overcome by a kind of demonic exultation; all our anger and distress found their outlet on Putli's body. Some of us kicked her corpse, some spit on her.'

What could be more undignified than that! But Putli was forced to become a *baghi* because of police torture. When she was a performer, high officials of the police force enjoyed her services for free, and after her death, they did not hesitate to kick or spit on her lifeless body. That day was one of the darkest days in the history of Indian police. It could have been one of their best, but that did not happen. No one got any information about Putli and Pahara's son, Surendra. But her daughter, her beloved Tanno, remained in Murena with her grandmother, Asgari Bai, to be exploited and abused by society. Later, one of the villagers informed me that both Asgari Bai and Putli's sister, Tara, tried their best to give Tanno a proper life. Finally, Tara Bai left for Kolkata with another person and took refuge in Sonagachi. She started living there and after Asgari Bai's death, she brought Tanno too to live with her.

After I returned from Chambal, I went to Sonagachi out

of my interest in the story and roamed around the area in search of Tanno. Beadon Street, Bowbazar, Harkata Gali, Rabindra Sarani—I walked around all these places, and after a long search, I got information about Putli Bai's daughter, Tanno. No, Tanno was no more in this world. Even Tara Bai was dead but my search had led me to a prostitute called Juthika who in turn told me about Jahnavi Devi. The middle-aged sex-worker had told me, 'Go to Jahnavi *masi*, the oldest resident of this area. She knows about everyone here. If anyone can provide you with information you want, it has to be her. If the old woman ignores you, take my name. I often buy her food. So there is a chance that she might help you out of gratitude.'

I found Jahnavi Das sitting on a porch in front of a house at the other end of Sonagachi. I went and sat beside her and asked, 'Do you know Tara Bai?' She stared at me for a while and then got worked up—'Who are you, the son of misfortune! You have come early in the morning to irritate me? No, I don't know anyone.' After a lot of coaxing, I managed to calm her down. I said, 'Oh grandmother, don't be angry. I have come to you only for some information. You are one of the oldest members of this place, so Juthika has asked me to come to you.' This pacified the old woman, and she said, 'You could have told me earlier that Juthika has sent you. She is a very good girl. Gets me food. But I shall not say anything. Give me something to eat first.' I went to the shop nearby and bought bread and eggs for her. She started eating and said, 'Now tell me what do you want to know.' I explained to her patiently that I wanted to know about a woman named Tara Bai who had come to Sonagachi from Chambal some 60 or 70 years ago. But it seemed that the old woman had never even heard of Chambal. I tried to explain again that she had come from Madhya Pradesh. She thought for a while and then said, 'Okay, understood. You are asking about Tara Rani, her elder sister's name was Putli Bai. I know her. She was my neighbour.' My perseverance had paid off. But the story that I heard from the old woman was in no way less thrilling than the narratives of Chambal.

Tara Bai came to Kolkata with an acquaintance and started staying at Sonagachi. She married that man and took the name Tara Rani. Later they shifted to Bowbazar. Putli Bai and Sultana Singh Tomar's daughter, Tanno, was brought up in Sonagachi. Whenever Tara entertained clients, Tanno stayed with this old woman whom she called *mashi*. She used to call Tara her mother. The daughter, too, had inherited her mother's beauty and youth. When she was 22, she fell in love with a young Muslim boy, a local goon, with whom she later eloped. She married him too. Jahnvi Devi had heard from Tara how Tanno, being a daughter of dacoits, was never accepted by society. She, too, had to become a victim of society. When the girl was around 10, they brought her to Calcutta. From a very early age, Tanno had seen how her society ill-treated her because of her parentage. That was one of the reasons why she fell in love with a Muslim man. Just after her wedding, Tanno brought her uncle and aunt to Bowbazar with her. What Jahnvi said after that was more shocking. 'Do you know the name of Tanno's son? You will not believe if I tell you, but blood always speaks. One can never deny the affection that blood relations have nor ignore the fault in one's bloodline.' I could not understand her and asked, 'What are you trying to say?' The toothless old woman laughed, 'Do you think I am saying all this just like that? The name of your Tanno's son is Rashid Khan, the one behind the Bowbazar bomb explosion.' Chewing on the piece of bread she kept muttering, 'Sin! Sin! How will you wipe it out from your blood! Wasn't he the grandson of two dacoits? I know everything.' But what was this old woman saying! The accused behind the bomb blast that took place in Bowbazar on 16 March 1993, Don Rashid Khan, was the grandson of Putli Bai! I was so taken aback by the revelation that I could not think any further. Giving some money to the old woman, I left that place. After reaching home I began researching Rashid Khan and took out old reports on him that were available online.

In the 1993 bomb blast at Bowbazar, 69 people had lost their lives. Rashid Khan and his five accomplices were apprehended. Not just the Bowbazar blast, Rashid Khan's name was associated with several crimes in Mumbai and other places. As my research proceeded, I became certain that Rashid Khan was Putli Bai's grandson. While in jail, he had a change of heart. He learnt to draw in prison. Then with police co-operation, there was an exhibition of his paintings in jail. Art, too, was in his blood. Time and surroundings had not been conducive to its manifestation. He utilised the period of his imprisonment and became a fine artist. His exhibition was well appreciated too. This seemed like a fairy-tale that went beyond mundane reality. Chambal, the tiny village of Barbai in Murena district, Kolkata's Sonagachi, and the Bowbazar blast—it was blood that brought all these places together. This was not an experience that I would forget soon. I thought that if I were to ever stop being a journalist, I would not have any regrets. The desire for adventure that had made me leave my IT profession and become a journalist, had been fulfilled by just this one trip to Chambal.

IN SEARCH OF THE BANDIT QUEENS

I took an early morning bus to Auria. It was 68 kilometres from Itawa, a journey of one and a half kilometres. This district has been the birthplace of three women dacoit leaders. Seema Parihar's house was in Bauni village in Auria. On another side of Auria was Mangalpuri which was the current address of Renu Yadav. And Neelam was living at Sarai Shishgaran. Seema had quit robbery a long time back, while Neelam and Renu had just come out of prison.

29 November 2003 was just like any other day. Renu Yadav of Jamalipur under Auria district had left her house for school. Just as she reached the outskirts of the village, the notorious dacoit of Chambal, Chandan Singh, kidnapped her. He asked her parents for 10 lakh rupees in exchange for her freedom. Renu's father was a poor farmer. He could not pay such a huge amount of ransom and get his daughter back. So Chandan gave Renu the title of his wife and kept her in the gang. Renu's school-life or adolescence soon turned into a life of thorny bushes in the *beeheds* of Chambal. Instead of books and pens, she was given deadly weapons that the gang had looted from the police. Though most of the dacoits had their eyes on Renu's attractive figure, they did not dare to harm her for fear of Chandan Singh. Many women

dacoits had embraced motherhood in the *beehed*. But none of them had drawn such attention as Renu Yadav. According to the sources, Renu sent her daughter to her parents' place in the hope of a better life and education. She did not want the shadow of Chambal to darken the life of her daughter. From the very beginning of her life in Chambal, almost all dacoit leaders desired Renu. The list included, Nirbhay Singh Gujjar, Chandan Garodiya, Gatta, and many more. At that time, because they were all scared of her so-called husband, Chandan Singh, they remained quiet, yet they secretly joined hands to try and find a way to get her.

Though most of the other leaders of the dacoit gangs stayed away from Renu, one of Chandan Singh's gang-members, Ramvir Gurjar, pumped multiple bullets into Chandan Singh's body one night, and ended his life. He thought that there would not be any more hindrances in his way of getting Renu. This incident took place on 5 January 2005. And around 10 days later another deadly incident shook Chambal. When deep in the night of 15 January 2005, Ramvir expressed his desire for Renu and tried to forcefully drag her to bed, she picked up the Self Loaded Rifle lying beside her, and fired all the shots at Ramvir. Thinking the enemy was dead, Renu fled from Chambal. But Ramvir was not dead, only gravely wounded. When he came to know that a few other dacoits of his gang had helped Renu escape, that very night he made three dacoits stand in a line, and shot them dead. He did this completely based on hunches, without any proof of their betrayal. So, once again, there was bloodshed in Chambal for a bandit beauty. Popular as the most beautiful and deadly dacoit of Chambal, Renu was scared for her life. She was under threat not from police or other authorities, but from the infamous dacoit Ramvir Gurjar—that same Ramvir who was once a drinking partner of Sardar Chandan Singh.

It was Renu's misfortune that Ramvir did not die. He is currently serving a sentence of life imprisonment. Renu has been constantly receiving threats from Ramvir and his cronies since the day she came out of her imprisonment. They said that if Renu did not return to Chambal, they were going to kill her. Uttar Pradesh police were providing her with security. After killing Ramvir, Renu ran around frantically in the *beehed* and after about a week finally reached Itawa. In various interviews, Renu has claimed that she surrendered to the police but the then Superintendent of Police, Daljit Singh Choudhary, has a different story to tell. He claims that Renu was arrested, along with the Self Loaded Rifle in her possession, by the police of Civil Lines police station. According to the police, Renu is not just extremely beautiful, but she also has a sharp brain. As long as she was in Chambal, the dacoits were so enamoured by her that they did not hesitate to kill each other for her. Neither the police nor the media had seen Renu when she was in Chambal, so there was a huge crowd just to see her during her trial.

Renu was five feet eleven inches tall, was slim, and had a charming face. Always dressed in a white shirt or t-shirt, blue jeans, and sports shoes, there was another thing that distinguished Renu—her way of speaking. According to the police, Renu's mouth was a steady source of abuses. Her vocabulary could easily put to shame both woman and men alike. Also, very few could match her in fighting or shooting. Renu had a weakness for Rayban sunglasses and expensive lipsticks. Her appearance was so attractive that most men were drawn towards her just after one glance. She was sent to jail on 14 February 2005. There were many cases filed against her under charges such as the Arms Act, looting, kidnapping, murder, and so on. After serving a term of seven years, on 29 May 2012, Renu was released from the Nari Niketan Open Jail in Lucknow. Though she was happy after her release, life outside Chambal became difficult for her. All the police officers, political leaders, or government officers who had forced Renu to sleep with them promising her a house, gun license, or police protection in return, began giving her a cold shoulder. After her release, Renu tried to lead an honourable life with support from a few political parties, but everywhere she received nothing more than empty words of comfort. Some producers showed interests in making films on her life, but unfortunately, even those did not work out. Renu also tried to work as a member of one of the cow protection committees, but even there the leering eyes of political leaders forced her to quit. When she tried to contest for Lok Sabha elections, luck failed her once again. By the time all her paperwork and formalities could be completed, the deadline was over. In an ironic twist of fate, Renu who had committed around 15 murders while in Chambal, had to warm the beds of police officials, leaders, and ministers—just to try and come back to normal life. But that, too, did not help her. Currently, Renu is, once again, contemplating returning to the *beehed*. And if she ends up going back there, will it be her fault?

Like Renu, Neelam too had been abducted one day while on her way to school. And it was in search for Neelam that I got down from the bus at a petrol pump in Auria. After getting off, I asked locals for directions to Sheeshgaran. One of them pointed at a trekker. The distance from Auria to Sheeshgaran was 25 kilometres. Travelling by the trekker, I kept thinking about Neelam's life—how a school-going girl of fifth standard became a dangerous dacoit. A woman *baghi* in the *beehed* has always been a cause for contention and bloodshed. Again and again, Chambal had become violent over the question of who would possess her. Many times the dacoits have been paid to abduct a girl because of some personal vendetta. And in later years such girls have turned into much-feared dacoits. Today Chambal seems quite peaceful. But even a few years back, it was not unusual to hear the tinkling of bangles and anklets accompanied by the jarring sound of gunshots. During my trip to Chambal, Uttar Pradesh elections were on, and I am told no dacoit came to cause trouble during the panchayat elections this time. They neither supported anyone nor forced villagers to cast their votes. However, it is relevant to mention here that this was the first panchayat election after police forces of Uttar Pradesh and Madhya Pradesh finished off most of the dacoit gangs. Bundelkhand, Itawa, Bhind, Murena—none of these places have shown threats from dacoits in the last election. Women dacoits have been particularly silent. Uttar Pradesh has seen too many such dangerous female dacoits.

After Putli Bai, Kusuma Nain was the most ferocious one. In the Chambal of the nineties, Kusuma was a name for terror. She remained the companion of the dacoit leader Ramasare alias Fakkar till the last day of her life. She belonged to Tikri village in Jalaon district. In 1978, Madho Singh, a dacoit belonging to Vikram Mallah's gang, had kidnapped Kusuma. When that gang split into two, she stayed with Lalaram's gang for a short period. But when Lalaram became close to Seema, a relationship developed between Kusuma and Nirbhay. She and Nirbhay left the group, and a few more dacoits accompanied them. But Kusuma could not stay for long with the womaniser, Nirbhay. She later fell in love with Fakkar and left with him to form a new gang. On the other side, Lalaram, after enjoying Seema's company for a long time, got her married to Nirbhay. Kusuma stayed with Fakkar for 10 long years before surrendering herself to Madhya Pradesh police in Bhind on 8 June 2004. She was still serving her term in jail during my trip to Chambal. Kusuma's deep love for Fakkar can be well understood from the following story. When in 2003-04, Fakkar fell so ill that he could not even hold his gun, Kusuma not only nursed him but remained with him like his shadow. During those days she had even saved him from several attacks by the police. Her softness for Fakkar was exactly opposed to her atrocities towards her enemies. The famous bandit queen Phoolan Devi had shot 22 men from the Thakur community at Behemai on 14 February 1981 to complete her revenge. Phoolan belonged to the Mallah or the Majhi community while Kusuma was born in a Thakur Family. To avenge the killing of so many Thakurs, Kusuma went to Maista village in Auria and following Phoolan made 13 Mallahs stand in a queue and shot them dead. That's not the end of her atrocities. She had plucked out the eyes of two members of their gang, Santosh and Rajbahadur, to punish them for betrayal. That day Kusuma wrote a new chapter of love and revenge in Chambal.

But Neelam Gupta and Sarala Jatav's stories were very different from those of these dacoit queens. After Mansingh, Mohar Singh, Malkhan, Gabbar, and other such dacoits, after the eighties, Chambal became home to a dacoit of a different kind. There were many women in his gang and all of them were real beauties. He had such an influence that he used to call the media to his den to give interviews. He had set up his parallel governance in more than 200 villages by selecting candidates who would contest elections from those areas. Whoever raised a voice was completely silenced. He was Nirbhay Singh Gurjar—one of the most notorious and Chambal's last dacoit of the old order. He was shot by the police in 2005. Neelam Gupta was the fourth wedded wife of Nirbhay. After serving a prison term of 13 years, she was released in January 2017, two months before my trip to Chambal. When Neelam was just 14, one of her father's enemies paid Nirbahay to kidnap her. Afterwards, Nirbhay retained her in the *beehed* and forced her to become a member of his gang. He married her on 28 February 2004. Later Neelam ran away with his adopted son, Shyam Jatav. There were several cases against Neelam. On 31 April 2004, Neelam surrendered at the Anti-Dacoit court in Itawah. She was sent to the women's Open Prison in Lucknow. On the very next day of her release from jail, Neelam had announced that she wanted to contest elections. But she could not decide the party from which she would contest. To narrate Neelam's story properly, it is important to talk about Nirbhay first. Otherwise, Neelam's story would remain incomplete.

In 1986, police arrested Nirbhay for petty theft and severely beat him up. As soon as he was released, he started planning his revenge and consequently joined the dacoit gang of Lalaram. Slowly Nirbhay became the most powerful person within the gang, the second-in-command of Lalaram. But he developed a relationship with Lalaram's partner, Kusuma Nain. When Lalaram came to know about this, he attacked Nirbhay. But Nirbhay escaped and formed a gang of his own. Gradually his terror increased in surrounding villages. He kept inducting more and more girls into his gang by kidnapping them. Seema Parihar, Munni Pandey, Parvati alias Chamko, Gauri Jatav, Sarala Jatav, and Neelam were chief among the women dacoits in his gang. Till 2005, there were around 250 dacoits in his gang. He had a different style of killing people. After murdering, he would cut off the nose, ear, or limb of the victim. There were around 200 murder cases and more than 350 charges of abduction against him. Before he was shot dead in 2005, there was a prize of 2.5 lakh on his head from the Madhya Pradesh and Uttar Pradesh police. Nirbhay's gang was well known because of its female members. He used to kidnap girls and then train them. Then the girls were forced to become a part of his gang. He had four legal marriages. His first wedded wife was Munni Pandey but she eloped with Munna Gurjar, the one whom Nirbhay considered his brother. He later found both of them and killed them as a punishment for betrayal. Then in 1986, Nirbhay married Seema Parihar. But she, too, could not stay with Nirbhay, the philanderer, and ran away with another dacoit. She surrendered in 2000. I have already mentioned Sarala while narrating Gauri's story. She was the daughter of the brother of Basanti, another of his wives. But Nirbhay was hurt the most by Neelam. Just six months after their wedding, she eloped with his adopted son, Shyam Jatav. While running away, she took around eight lakh rupees in cash, jewellery worth four lakh, and many weapons. Before marrying Neelam, Nirbhay got Shyam married to Sarala, but that was just for show. In reality, Nirbhay continued his pleasure with Sarala as before. Neelam made use of this opportunity to seduce Shyam. She slowly kept instigating him against Nirbhay. One day, when they got the opportunity, they eloped. Nirbhay was beside himself with anger and declared a prize of 21 lakh rupees for anyone who could catch Neelam. Thereafter, Nirbhay married Sarala. This 16-year-old girl continued to run the gang long after Nirbhay's death. Nirbhay's attitude had numbered his days—on one hand was his debauchery, and on the other, his extreme desire to join politics. In 2005, when Nirbhay was killed in police encounter, Samajwadi Party was in power in Uttar Pradesh. Mulayam Singh Yadav was Chief Minister. At that time Nirbhay's terror was at its peak in Itawah and its adjoining areas. The Opposition always brought allegations against Mulayam Singh Yadav and his brother, Shivpal Yadav, for sheltering the dacoits of Chambal. Around this time Nirbhay held a press conference at his den and openly addressed Shivpal as his elder brother. He also said that they were constantly in touch. The Opposition, particularly Mayawati's party, created a lot of ruckus about it. Anger, greed, lust, and craving for power were the chief enemies of Nirbhay. Shivpal was not at all happy with Nirbhay's statement to the media. That was the beginning of 'Operation Nirbhay.' A Special Taskforce was engaged to end Nirbhay. STF killed almost 40 members of his gang. The elopement of Neelam and Shyam had added further problems for the gang. They passed information regarding the gang's activities to STF. Both of them had surrendered to the STF. Finally, on 8 November 2005, Neelam informed the STF about a meeting that was supposed to take place between Nirbhay and a businessman in the Chatarpur region. The STF killed Nirbhay in an encounter there. However, like every other instance, this time too the police and STF refused to acknowledge receiving any help from Neelam. It is true that without her help police could never have found Nirbhay.

When Nirbhay abducted Neelam from Bidhuna in Auria in 2001, she was only 14. Nirbhay used to force himself on her and there was no escape for her from that place. So, she slowly started adapting herself to the ways of Nirbhay's gang. There was also the rule of Chambal that wherever a gang committed robbery, they used to leave a chit with names of all the gang members to ensure that no one leaves the gang. Therefore, Neelam's name was already involved with the gang. She started bringing a change in her attire as well—jeans and a t-shirt with an open breast shirt tied in a knot at the waist. She sported a red *bindi*, a belt of bullets on her shoulders, and a rifle. This was how she appeared in the media. There were numerous pictures, YouTube videos, etc where she appeared in this way. At times, she was even seen tying Nirbhay's long hair. Shyam Jatav had also been kidnapped by Nirbhay but later Nirbhay started acknowledging him as his son.

My trekker reached Shishgaran. I was confounded after getting down at the highway. On either side of the road, there was the village and a few farms. Even after asking around in the nearby houses, I could not get any lead regarding Neelam. No one could even say whether anyone by the name of Neelam Gupta even lived there. After trying for almost an hour I decided to return to Auria. Once again, I took a trekker back to that petrol pump in Auria. I saw a small tea shop there and went inside. As I was trying to plan my next step, I saw two policemen entering the shop. I was hopeful—they must know the current address of Neelam Gupta. I went and introduced myself to them. They were Baburam Gurjar, around 50 years of age, and Vikas Singh who was in his mid-thirties. After listening to my query, one of them said, 'Are you talking about that Neelam who was Nirbhay's mistress? That slut stays here only.' I was shocked by the language of these policemen. I protested, 'But Baburamji, wasn't she the wedded wife of Nirbhay!' He laughed aloud, 'What are you talking about, Bangali babu! Forget about these *beehed* marriages, the truth is that she is a known slut. Yes, she had indeed been kidnapped but she too had created a lot of nuisance. Who would otherwise do all these things with a foster son?' There was no point in talking to them anymore and hence I asked if they knew her current address. Baburam said, 'Neelam lives quite nearby. There is a Ramlila ground if you cross this petrol pump and take a left. Her brother, Manish Gupta, runs a small *paan*-shop across that ground. Neelam and her mother are presently staying with him.' Thanking them and paying my bills I left the tea shop. The conversation had left a bad after-taste. After walking for about 10 minutes, I saw a large ground and located a shop nearby. A woman was sitting there. I enquired her about Neelam. She in turn asked me where I was coming from. When I told her about myself, she sent a message. By then an old woman had arrived as well. She was Neelam's mother. She offered me a bottle of an aerated drink from her shop. We started conversing on various topics. After almost half an hour, Neelam and her brother joined us. Manish arranged two chairs for us from a nearby storehouse. The interview started. The photograph of Neelam that I had come across, she was barely 14 or 15. Now she was a young woman of 30 years. She was much smarter than her YouTube version; and was also more cautious, and careful while speaking. I was encountering a Neelam who was ambitious, smart and prepared to brush aside all allegations against her.

Author: So, when were you released from jail?

Neelam: Almost four months back.

A: The newspapers reported that you were released in January.

N: See, the orders regarding my release had come from the Juvenile court on 26 November 2016. But there were a few more pending cases. Hence it got delayed.

A: How did you reach Nirbhay Gurjar's gang?

N: That's a story known to everyone, still I am repeating for you. I was a student at Saraswati Gyan Mandir, a school in Bidhuna. One day I was abducted on my way to school.

A: Who kidnapped you?

N: Some people from my village who had some enmity with my family. They got Nirbhay's gang to kidnap me.

A: When did you first take up gun?

N: I did not. It was much later that I had to carry it for the sake of my security. Initially, I did not have any idea about these things. I was also scared of guns. I was too young for such things. Three months had passed since my abduction. Nirbhay kept trying to teach me how to shoot. I refused to learn in spite of his scoldings and threats. But one day when I tried to help the police, believing that I could save myself that way, the police started firing at me! Then I realised how important it was to learn shooting to survive there.

A: How many kinds of guns are you familiar with?

N: I know how to use a rifle, light machine gun, pistol, and country-made pistols. When I finally learnt to shoot, I was the best in Nirbhay's gang. A crack-shot! (She added with a laugh)

A: How many crimes have you committed after you joined the gang?

N: (After staying quiet for some time) I did not commit any crime. Let me tell you the truth, like all other dacoit leaders, Nirbhay had a letter-pad too. During any crime, he used to write the names of all the members of the gang and leave the list at the site of action so that none of us could ever leave.

Everyone in the gang lived in fear that if anyone leaves the *beehed*, either the person will get arrested or die in a police encounter. I had never accompanied them in their kidnapping missions. It used to be done by other gang members. There used to be *bichliya*, agents with the gang. They used to do the kidnapping. Nirbhay had kidnapped many people during my stay with the gang. See, I was never interested in these things. While I was in the *beehed*, my only thought was to find a way to escape from that place. And secondly, Nirbhay never shared his secrets with anyone. So, I have never committed any crime.

A: Have you ever killed any person by your own hands or committed any robbery?

N: (With bowed head) No. I have never killed anyone and never robbed. (There are around 10 murder cases and 70 charges of abduction against Neelam.)

A: Everyone knows that you were married to Nirbhay. Where did the wedding take place?

N: At Peepalgaria—a village in the Chambal valley. We got married at the temple of *Siddh Baba* there.

A: Why did you run away with Shyam?

N: Shyam was my only way to escape from there. So, I befriended him.

A: How was your relationship with Shyam?

N: Like with a friend.

A: In an interview during your surrender, you said that you had married Shyam.

N: (She got agitated on hearing this and cut me short) Of course not. Shyam's wife is Sarala Jatav.

A: But that interview shows both you and Sarala sitting together outside the Itawah court. Sarala was asked the same question and she said in front of you that both of you were in a romantic relationship and that you had secretly married him.

N: This is wrong. Absolutely wrong. There is a proverb in Hindi that the one who is drowning would clutch even at a straw. Shyam was that straw for me. He knew the forest much more than I did because he had been staying there since he was nine years old. Nirbhay had kidnapped him from Delhi. I supported Shyam so that he could tell me the way out of that forest.

A: Did you ever injure anyone?

N: No. But I was myself injured by police bullets. In a 2003 confrontation with the police, my shoulder was hit by a bullet.

A: What kind of behaviour did you face from the police and other prisoners?

N: Initially the police looked down upon all the inmates, called all of us criminals. But during my stay there, due to my behaviour, their attitude improved. My relationship with other women prisoners was also quite good. Kusuma Nain had even touched my head to bless me. Renu had become a good friend. I had also met Mohar Singhji and Malkhan Singhji a few times at the Itawah court. They too had given me their blessings.

A: What are your plans for the future?

N: There are two film directors, Krishna Mishra and Girija Shanker Agarwal from Jalaon who have expressed their wishes to make a movie on my life and cast me in the lead role. But the conversation is at an early stage. Let's see what comes out of it.

A: While in jail you had sent a letter to Akhilesh Yadav, the Chief Minister of Uttar Pradesh. What did you write in the letter?

N: I had written to him thrice, complaining against the injustice that I was facing. I asked him for his help but nothing happened. I was awarded life imprisonment. I was just 15 then. It is said that at that age the juvenile court does not pass a sentence against anyone. But I had to complete my jail term. I was away from my family for 13 years. During that period my father passed away and I could not even see him for the last time. My whole family was ruined. For me, my mother, too, had to serve a term in prison because the police did not want anyone to be a support for me. While I was in jail, Nirbhay had threatened that he would kill anyone who helped me. This warning was especially for my family. The police then arrested my mother so that she could not meet me. My father was already dead and my brothers had to live in hiding. Still one of my brothers helped them to catch Kallu and put him in jail. These people were never in the gang, in fact, they were not even remotely connected to it. Still, same charges were brought against them—of abductions.

A: What kind of a person was Nirbhay?

N: What can I say about him! A horrid rascal! (Getting excited) He was a philanderer. There is no count of the number of rapes he had committed. He did not even leave girls who were young enough to be his daughters. There is a saying that never judge a book by its cover. It fits Nirbhay. He presented a good image of himself to the world—helping to get girls married, giving away his wealth in charity, and so on. But all these were for show. In reality, he preyed upon those very girls whom he helped to get married. I do not have words enough to express the extent of his depravity. He abducted Sarala and then got her married to Shyam. That makes Sarala his daughter-in-law. But I have seen Nirbhay in inappropriate positions with her. And Sarala, too, was such a woman. She kept her affair with Nirbhay. I hope you can now very well guess what kind of a person Nirbhay was.

A: Did you quarrel with Nirbhay regarding Sarala?

N: Yes, many times. I told him 'If you want to bed Sarala, why did you spoil my life?'

A: What was his reply?

N: What will a rascal reply! He always said, 'I do whatever I wish to. I am the *Sardar*, I can get anything done at gunpoint.'

A: What were the other vices of Nirbhay?

N: He used to drink a lot and forced us to drink as well. Sarala enjoyed drinking. But I had to be forced to do so. After that, we had to dance in front of him. He said that he liked girls who drank and smoked, and he enjoyed them in bed more. After a while, I too got addicted to cigarettes, opium, and alcohol. We had to dance in a state of drunkenness and after that do his bidding. Once he tried to force me and Sarala on the same bed, but I did not agree. How could I agree to such a thing! Since then, my resolve to run away became stronger.

A: You said a few days back that you wanted to join politics.

N: Yes, I am working towards that. I want to be like Seema Parihar and Phoolan Devi.

A: Which political party would you like to join?

N: See, I have said previously too that there are two parties that I admire—one is Modiji's BJP and the other is Akhileshji's Samajwadi Party.

A: Between these two which would you like to join?

N: To tell you the truth, if I get an offer from both parties then it will be very difficult for me to choose. Therefore, I have left that to time. However much one praises Modi, it will be less. His work for our country has made everyone—all old, young, and children, his fan. And the impression that

Akhileshji has built for himself in the entire of Uttar Pradesh is unparalleled. So, to choose any one among these is beyond my capability. I am researching both of them and have left everything to fate.

I found Neelam's actions during our conversation quite peculiar. She slowly drew the chair too close to me. As she spoke, she also kept stroking my hand. She said, 'You are like a friend to me. You have come from such a distant place to take my interview! You are in the media, you are powerful—do something for me. I shall also show you my *jalwa*, my charisma.' Then she started tickling my ears. I felt uncomfortable. The godown was in semi-darkness and there was no one around. A low-power CFL was the only source of light in the room where I was speaking to Neelam. I perceived that things were not going in the right direction. Neelam was keen to leave Chambal. She wanted to join politics or get a chance in movies at any cost. And she was willing to do anything for that. Chambal had taught her that her body and her beauty were her biggest weapon and she could gain a lot using them.

During the conversation, she said that she was not keen to get married and start anew. She had somehow managed the friendship of quite an influential person in Varanasi. Neelam's words hinted that they were not just friends but more. So even if the BJP or the Samajwadi Party ignored her, she would have other means of joining politics. That person also helped her in procuring a few firearms. Even while we were talking there was a pistol lying on her lap. Hence, I was not allowed to take her photograph. Though my hands were itching to shoot one picture, I was helpless. Later I found out that my intuitions were not wrong. Just before I started writing this book, I received the news that Neelam was contesting in the 2018 municipal elections. She was contesting for the seat of the chairperson from Itawah, the area that was known as the stronghold of Mulayam Singh Yadav.

I had never felt any problem with Mansingh, Mohar

Singh, or Seema Parihar joining politics. But I had ardently wished that Neelam should not contest elections and even if she did, she should not win. While talking to her mother, brother, and sister-in-law, I had realised that they were extremely dangerous people. And Neelam was even more dangerous. Once she gets access to power, she would unleash terror. She could become completely autocratic. Added to it was her limitless greed. Nirbhay was a vicious and lustful person. But early exposure to the lawlessness of Chambal, alcohol, and opium, have turned Neelam into a person even worse than Nirbhay. If such a person got access to power, hell would break loose. She was the one to stroke Nirbhay's desire for political power. And that ambition for power was very much evident in Neelam even while she was in Chambal. In Nirbhay's absence, Sarala remained in charge of the gang. She was also the one responsible for distributing the loot. Cunning Neelam could not accept that. Without anyone's knowledge, she developed a physical relationship with Shyam. She was so manipulative and clever that the other cunning woman, Sarala, did not get a whiff of it. Slowly, she got Shyam completely in her power. Not just Shyam, she established physical relationships with several other powerful members of the gang to strengthen her position. At that time many local political leaders used to come to Nirbhay's den to seek his help during elections. Under Nirbhay's command, Sarala and Neelam had to entertain those leaders. Neelam used that time to developed relationship with a number of them even beyond Nirbhay's instructions. On the other hand, Shyam, though considered Nirbhay's son, was not getting the command of the gang. His wife, too, had become his father's mistress. The only distraction that life in *beehed* offered was alcohol and opium. In such a situation he could not ignore Neelam's advances. Like a fool, he had given himself up to her completely and Neelam too kept using him. Initially, she instigated him against Sarala and Nirbhay. Then she used him to come out of the *beehed*, taking away a lot of money from the gang, jewellery that the gang had looted, and also the ones that belonged to Sarala. The weapons they stole from the gang could not be recovered by police even today. Who knows whether the pistol lying on Neelam's lap during the interview was one of those!

Neelam, Renu Yadav and Kusuma Nain were in the same jail. She befriended both of them and got information about the who's who of Uttar Pradesh. The first thing she did after coming out of jail was to get in touch with them. And then she started presenting herself to the media as a helpless woman. She had been reiterating the same thing again and again—that she had been abused and exploited, that she had never been associated with any criminal activities like murder, abduction, etc. All these were gross lies. It was also a lie that the police had arrested her mother and brother without any reason because even while she was in Chambal, one of her brothers was in regular contact with Kallu. She used to steal robbed items from the gang and sneak them out of the *beehed* with the help of her brother. She has very easily used her body to get closer to that influential person from Varanasi and used him to procure a party ticket for herself. Even though she keeps proclaiming her innocence, many videos on the internet show her shooting in Chambal. There are about 20 murder cases against her and about 35 to 40 cases of abduction. There are charges of robberies too. Quite a number of these charges were proved in court. She did not even leave Shyam who had helped her out of the *beehed*. As soon as she came out, she told on him and got him implicated. Today Neelam says that she wants to stop violence against women. But I cannot trust her words. Women like Phoolan Devi or Seema Parihar had joined politics a long time back but none of their attitudes were like that of Neelam. On the other hand, Renu Yadav was even more dangerous than Neelam. Whenever Sarala spoke, she rained abuses. They too wanted to join politics, but not at the cost of their self-respect.

Neelam kept telling me, 'You have travelled a long distance. It will take time to return to Auria. We could not show our hospitality towards you. Stay here for the night and you will not regret it.' It was not very difficult to understand the meaning behind her words. Just a while back, I was upset with Baburam's words. During this trip across Chambal, the attitude of the police had often disturbed me. But perhaps they were not always wrong. Neelam told me that she had written a book on her life in the *beehed* in the form of a diary. I asked her to show that to me to which she said that she would charge me for that. I smiled at her words. I knew that most of the things written by her would be fabricated tales where she would try to pass herself as an innocent person. That's how she had presented herself in all her recent interviews. Ironically, when Neelam had surrendered and was brought to court thereafter, she was proud of her life in the *beehed*. It used to reflect in her appearance as well as words. In spite of all these, I was curious about her diary. She had later called up her brother and asked him to bring the diary. I read most of it; it was written in Hindi and in poor handwriting. But it certainly had some value. There were detailed and interesting descriptions of life in the *beehed* and operations of dacoits. But the problem was in those places where she was talking about herself—they were mostly concocted. At least that's what my research told me. The same thing had been said by a couple of dacoits from Nirbhay's gang. Neelam's terror during her *beehed* days was unbelievable. No other woman dacoit had been as cunning and unabashed as her. Added to it was her fiery temper. It was in a fit of one such temper that she had once killed a child, who had been abducted by the gang, by throwing the child to the ground. If this book ever comes out as an autobiography of the life of a female bandit, a large part of it would remain a lie. Still, this book, being authored by a dreaded female dacoit, will be a significant work. I did not wish to continue my conversation with her any further. I had gathered all that I wanted to know and had no interest in prolonging the discourse. I got up from there and waited for the return bus.

RETURN

The next morning was my return journey. I would go back to Kolkata, my regular life, leaving Chambal behind. I kept thinking about Chambal and its people on my way back to Itawah by bus. Itawah and its surroundings were quite developed now. There was a Lion Safari Park nearby and many more such places that drew tourists. But beyond and above everything, I was overwhelmed by the *baghis* and their lives in the *beehed*. There were so many stories and each story had so many twists and turns. For a few days, I was surrounded by their lives, their struggles, their happiness, and their sorrow. It would not be possible to pen down all the stories that are there in my mind. I could not include everything in this book, a lot remains untold. I could not write about many people—some *baghis* too were left out.

There have been so many names associated with *baghis*. Once there was a *baghi* by the name of Sultana. Jim Corbett himself helped the police catch him. But even Jim Corbett was extremely displeased with the attitude of the police towards these *baghis* and he had written a long letter to his friend, a high police official in those days. Many of us are already familiar with this story from *Abhisapta Chambal* and *Beehed, Baghi, Bandook.* A hunter like Jim Corbett too was impressed by the courage of *baghis*. He had wanted the law to acknowledge the bravery of these people and punish them accordingly. He did not support police injustice on them. Jim Corbett, Tarun Bhaduri, and many such men have seen *baghis* from a close quarter and had even participated in their lifestyle. I too have gathered many gems from my trip to Chambal.

The bus had already reached the stop near my hotel. I retired for the night. But however hard I tried, sleep eluded me. I was too excited to sleep. It was a different kind of excitement. I could not sleep the night I had boarded Ananya Express to reach Chambal because of my eagerness to see the place. But the present day's excitement also carried in itself a lot of hesitation. It was a tussle to understand who was right and who was in the wrong, who was innocent and who was to be blamed. Most of these *baghis* are heroes in their tribes. To others, these very people were synonymous to terror. I couldn't judge them. They too had their own opinions regarding their crimes. It would not be possible for city dwellers like us to understand their perspectives. Their grief, their struggles were very different from ours. It was altogether a different experience to hear them, to see their lives. I can only present stories of their sufferings. I can take their tales of exploitation, deprivation, and injustice to my readers. I can tell the story of a minor soldier, Paan Singh Tomar, who earned medals for his country at the international level and how he only had to fight against the landlords of his village to save his land from them. But when he failed to do so, the soldier who was once fighting for the country, turned into a dangerous *baghi*. He had to choose *beehed* and he picked up the gun to save his family. This has been the timeless tale of Chambal, its tradition. Otherwise, why would soldiers like Madho Singh or Paan Singh Tomar choose to become a *baghi* in the *beehed*? And why should Madho Singh, after his surrender, spend life in ignominy, performing magic shows on streets to earn a livelihood in his final days? Why would the *beehed* draw women like Gauri Jatav, who had dreams of getting educated and helping her parents after finding a job? No historian or research scholars have till date found the reason as to why the *beehed* sucked these hard-working people into its fold. And how can they do so! Chambal has its own rules. Here they kill for revenge, to protest against rapes, to fight against injustice, or even to save the land. It was carrying the curse of Mahabharata even in the 21st century. I wonder if it will ever end.

The *baghis* who fought for a cause are all gone. Their places have been taken by dacoits. Perhaps some other set of people would come to take their place someday. Look at Ram Singh or Guchcha Singh, working in these hotels. Even in 2017, Ram has to fight against the law to regain his land. Where is the justice for people like him? The people of Chambal have too many enemies to fight and they are alone, helpless. On one side are their enemies, on the other, there is the law, and added to it is the curse of Chambal. They have to constantly fight against three formidable opponents. And when they lose, the *beehed* sucks them in. The *beehed* in Chambal lies in waiting like a sly fox. It keeps watching for the rise of enmity or a voice that screams against injustice—and at the slightest pretext, the *beehed* would pull them into its terrain, and make a cruel, dreaded *baghi* out of them.

It was already morning. I packed my luggage and checked out of the hotel. The train was due in some time. I booked an auto from the hotel itself and left for the station. The train arrived a little later than its scheduled time. I took my place in it—side lower berth. Perhaps I have not been able to say everything properly in this book. If I get a chance again someday, I would write again. But some things will always remain unsaid. These 14 days in Chambal has changed my perspective towards life in many ways. The train gathered speed. Slowly Chambal, the *beehed*, the *baghis* started fading, and I left behind Mansingh, Lukka, Mohar, Malkhan, Renu, Neelam.

The *beehed* in Chambal. Photo by Suvendu Debnath.

The escape route for Malkhan Singh. Photo by Suvendu Debnath.

Chambal—believed to be most transparent yet cursed river in India. Photo source: internet.

The mysterious fort of Ater. Photo source: internet.

Hands-on training. Mohor Singh guides Bholu for the rifle.
Photo by Suvendu Debnath.

Photograph of Malkhan Singh by Suvendu Debnath.

Malkhan Singh met the journalists after he surrendered.
Photo source: internet.

The *garhi* of Mansingh. Photo by Suvendu Debnath.

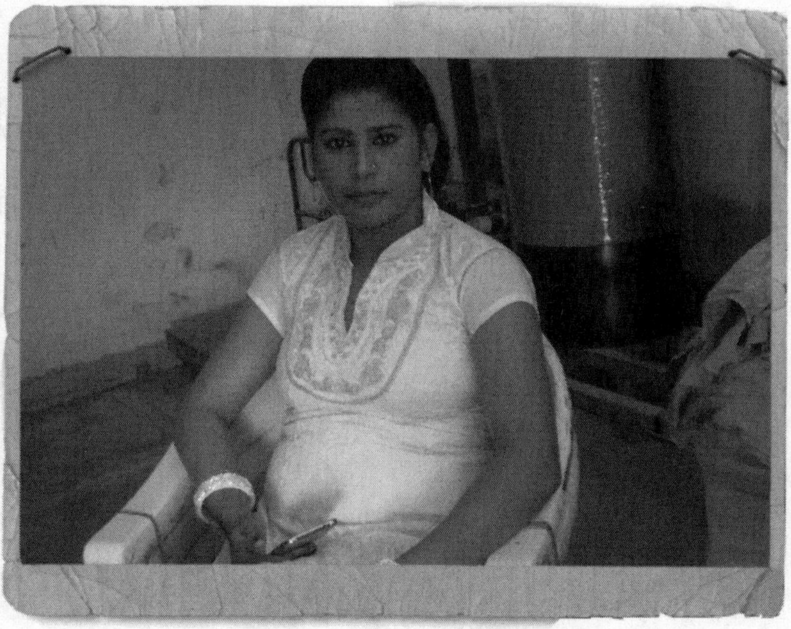

Photograph of Neelam Gupta by Suvendu Debnath.

Photograph of Renu Yadav — source: internet.

Neelam Gupta being brought to the court. Photo source: internet.

Naresh Singh at the temple of Mansingh.
Photo by Suvendu Debnath.

GLOSSARY

Akhada — wrestling arena

Batasha — a sort of Indian sugar drops also used for religious purposes. Often made from jaggery too

Bajre ki roti and sukhi saag — Indian handmade millet flatbread and dried greens

Dhol — an Indian percussion

Gomedh yajna — an ancient Hindu ritual

Garhi — fort

Ghungroo — anklets used particularly in the traditional Indian dance forms

Ghomta — veil

Giroh — gang

Gamcha — a cotton cloth used as a bath towel across India

Jhola — a side bag

Kotha — traditional centres where mujras (a form of entertainment using song and dance) are performed

Khap panchayat — a community of elders of a particular tribe or clan who solve disputes. They do not have any official position but wield a lot of power.

Kund — a water body or reservoir

Lota — a traditional Indian rounded water pot

Nagara — a type of Indian percussion

Patrakar — journalist

Sarfaroshi ki tamanna — a popular patriotic song in Hindi

Saali — a kind of slang used both as abuse and endearment

Tasha — a musical instrument